OSPREY COMBAT AIRCRAFT • 28

AIR WAR IN THE FALKLANDS

1982

SERIES EDITOR: TONY HOLMES

OSPREY COMBAT AIRCRAFT • 28

AIR WAR IN THE FALKLANDS 1982

Christopher Chant

Front Cover
In the late afternoon (17.04 hours) on 1 May 1982, one of two Sea Harrier FRS.Mk 1 aircraft (serial number XZ451, identification code 000) of 801 Squadron used an AIM-9L Sidewinder AAM to shoot down a Canberra B.Mk 62 (serial B-110) of *Grupo 2 de Bombardeo,* flying a south-easterly course over the South Atlantic with no land in sight, head-on at a range of about 8,000 yards (7,300 m) during an engagement at about 36,000 ft. Two other Canberras had broken off on sighting the two Harriers.

First published in Great Britain in 2001 by Osprey Publishing
Elms Court, Chapel Way, Botley, Oxford, OX2 9LP
E-mail: info@ospreypublishing.com

Reprinted 2003

ISBN 1841762938

Page design by TT Designs, T & B Truscott
Aircraft Profiles by Mark Rolfe
Cover Artwork by Keith Woodcock
Origination by Grasmere Digital Imaging, Leeds, UK
Printed through Bookbuilders, Hong Kong

03 04 05 10 9 8 7 6 5 4 3 2

Photo Credits. All photos courtesy of MARS except: Argentine air force (36, 37 bottom, 42, 44, 45, 48, 51 bottom, 66 top, 72, 76 and 77); Argentine navy (10, 32-33, 35 bottom, 37 top, 52, 53 top, 54, 55, 57, 58, 62 bottom and 63); British Aerospace (title page, 26, 41 and 82); Paul A. Jackson (11 bottom); Dr. Alfred Price (39, 70 and 81)

CONTENTS

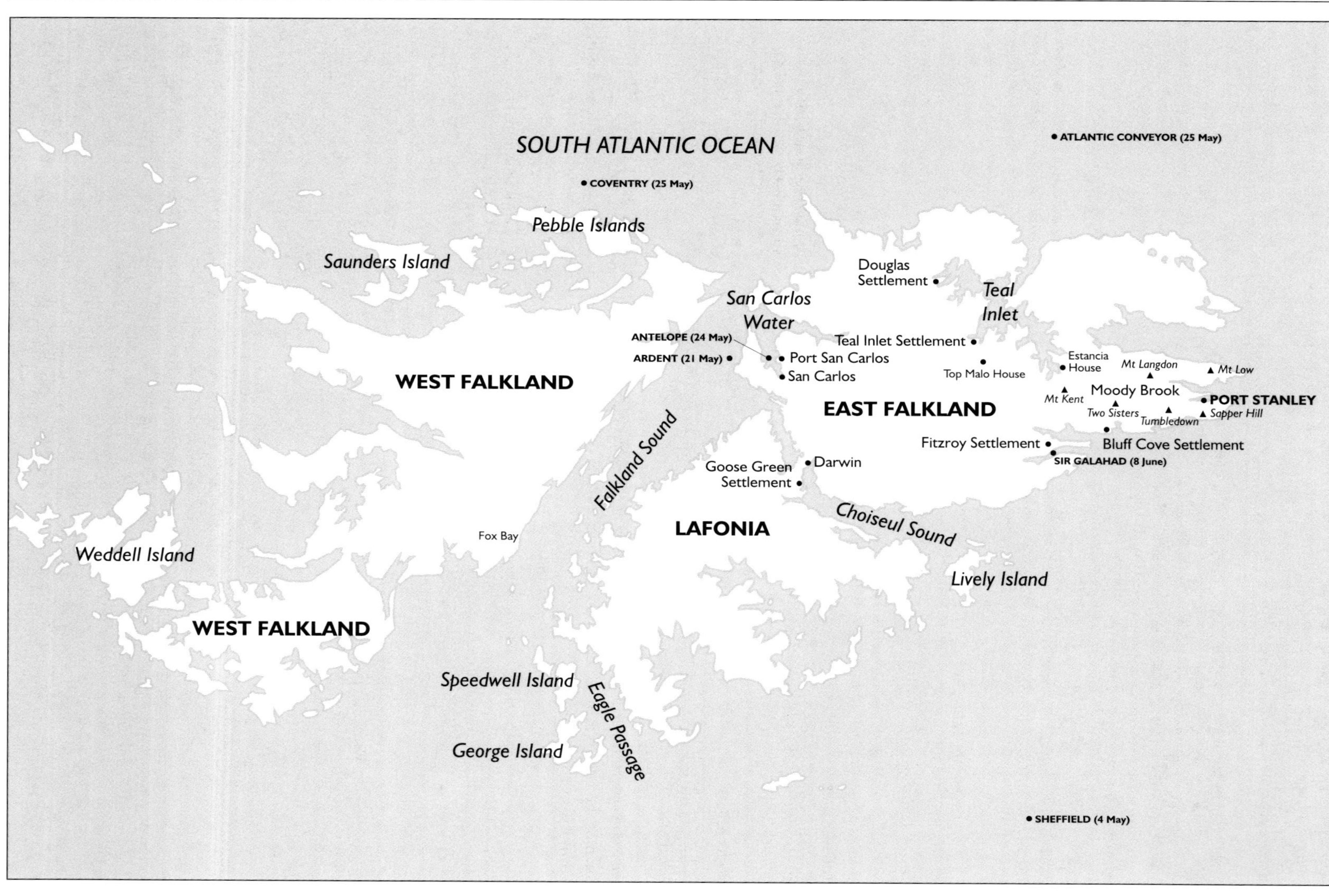
SOUTH ATLANTIC OCEAN
ATLANTIC CONVEYOR (25 May)
COVENTRY (25 May)
Pebble Islands
Saunders Island
Douglas Settlement
San Carlos Water
Teal Inlet
ANTELOPE (24 May)
ARDENT (21 May)
Port San Carlos
San Carlos
Teal Inlet Settlement
Top Malo House
Estancia House
Mt Langdon
Mt Low
WEST FALKLAND
Mt Kent
Moody Brook
PORT STANLEY
EAST FALKLAND
Two Sisters
Tumbledown
Sapper Hill
Fitzroy Settlement
Bluff Cove Settlement
SIR GALAHAD (8 June)
Goose Green Settlement
Darwin
Falkland Sound
LAFONIA
Choiseul Sound
Fox Bay
Weddell Island
Lively Island
WEST FALKLAND
Speedwell Island
Eagle Passage
George Island
SHEFFIELD (4 May)

ERROR COMPOUNDS ERROR

Between April and June 1982, a small campaign was fought between British and Argentine air, sea and land forces for control of the Falkland Islands, a small group of islands lying many thousands of miles from the United Kingdom in the South Atlantic only a few hundreds of miles off the coast of Argentina, which knew the islands as the Islas Malvinas. This Falklands war has been the most recent military operation undertaken by the United Kingdom not in partnership with one or more allies, and remains a clear object lesson of the importance of well-handled air power as an arbiter of associated sea and land campaigns. Indeed, it is arguable that without the availability of carrierborne warplanes the British would have been foolhardy even to undertake the campaign, in which the tactical success of the British Aerospace Sea Harrier multi-role fighters of the Fleet Air Arm, operating from two aircraft carriers, made it possible for the ships of the Royal Navy and the men of the British army to complete the operation to retake the islands from Argentine occupation.

The question of sovereignty over the Falkland Islands has been disputed between the United Kingdom and Argentina since 1833, the year in which a British naval vessel arrived at the islands, expelled a small

Seen on the metal planking of an airstrip improvised on the soft surface of East Falkland, this is a Harrier GR.Mk 3 close support warplane of the Royal Air Force's No. 1 Squadron. The aeroplane carries drop tanks and launchers for 68-mm (2.68-in) SNEB air-to-surface unguided rockets. With cannon fire and bombs, these were the most important weapons delivered by the Harrier, whose long nose carried a laser rangefinder and marked-target seeker for use in the delivery of the laser-guided bombs that were used only in small numbers

number of Argentine settlers and formally laid claim to the islands for the United Kingdom. The disputed claim to the islands was discussed from time to time between representatives of the two countries, but in overall terms little if any real progress toward a solution of the problem was found. A military government under the leadership of General Leopoldo Galtieri assumed control of Argentina during 1977, and in 1978 the British government despatched a small naval task force to the South Atlantic after receiving intelligence information that the Argentines were possibly planning the occupation of South Georgia, the main island of a south-eastern dependency of the Falklands.

At this time, during the later part of the 1970s, the United Kingdom's defence posture seemed to have stabilised after a protracted period of strategic imbalance resulting from a general inability, or perhaps reluctance, by a succession of British governments to appreciate fully the implications of the United Kingdom's decline as a world power. In more recent years, though, there had emerged a number of new policies reflecting the realities of a switch from a world to a European focus. This switch in emphasis had been caused ultimately by the inability of the United Kingdom to finance a continued world commitment, but even so and despite the various defence cuts that typified political and economic thinking during the 1960s and 1970s, expenditure on the British defence budget was still comparatively high by comparison with that of most European nations. When a Conservative government was elected in 1979, though, there was a widening chasm between what the nation could sensibly afford in economic terms and what was required for the satisfaction of current defence commitments.

Pride and joy of the Argentine navy and here seen in 1980, the carrier ARA *Veinticinco de Mayo* (25 May, Argentina's national day) was built in the second half of World War II as HMS *Venerable* of the 'Colossus' class of light carriers, and in 1948 passed to Dutch ownership as HrMS *Karel Doorman*. Argentina bought the ship in October 1958 and took her over after a major refit (including the installation of an angled flight deck and a steam catapult) in a Dutch yard. The flightdeck was enlarged in 1980-81, allowing two additional aircraft to be parked on the deck, and changes were effected to allow the ship's embarkation of Super Etendard attack fighters ordered from France

Laid down in June 1944 but launched only in February 1953 for commissioning in November 1959, the aircraft carrier HMS *Hermes* had a long British career (including service as a commando carrier in 1973-76 and anti-submarine carrier from 1977) before being sold to India in 1985 for continuing service as INS *Viraat.* The flight deck was revised with a 'ski jump' forward section in 1980 allowing the embarkation of five Sea Harrier aircraft and nine Sea King helicopters, increased for the Falklands campaign to 12 Sea Harrier and 18 Sea King machines

The result, almost inevitably, was a defence review whose results were offered to Parliament in June 1981 by the Secretary of State for Defence, John Nott. Known as 'The United Kingdom Defence Programme: The Way Forward', this review saw the only way of eliminating the chasm was the removal of virtually all of the country's remaining global aspirations so that defence orientation could be aligned more fully and effectively to the North Atlantic Treaty Organisation's (NATO's) primary area of concern, namely Europe and the threat posed by the possibility of aggression by the USSR and its Warsaw Pact allies. The roles and equipment of the British army and the Royal Air Force (RAF) had been directed

Armed with 30-mm cannon and AIM-9L Sidewinder air-to-air missiles, and also carrying two drop tanks, a Sea Harrier FRS.Mk 1 (possibly XZ496 of No. 800 Squadron) hovers over the flight deck of HMS *Hermes.* In the foreground are pairs of free-fall bombs as yet unfitted with their tail units

toward a European focus for some time already, so the implications of the defence review inevitably fell most acutely on the Royal Navy. With a view to making a major contribution to the NATO defence of the eastern Atlantic and the English Channel, there would henceforward be two rather than three aircraft carriers, and the supporting forces of destroyers and frigates would be trimmed from 59 to some 50 ships. Given the smaller number of warships that would now exist, the Royal Fleet Auxiliary, tasked with resupply of warships at sea, would also be reduced in size, dockyards would be scaled down in capability or even closed, and a manpower reduction of some 10,000 persons could be expected.

It soon began to become clear what the effect of these changes would be in the composition and capabilities of the Royal Navy's surface strength. The service's two amphibious assault ships, HMS *Fearless* and HMS *Intrepid,* were to be placed in reserve, the new small aircraft carrier HMS *Invincible* was offered to Australia (but rejected), and the anti-submarine carrier HMS *Hermes* was to be taken out of service. At lower levels of the Royal Navy's overall capabilities the full gamut of support facilities was reduced, and orders were issued for the ice-patrol ship HMS *Endurance,* which was the United Kingdom's sole naval vessel permanently deployed to the South Atlantic, to sail for home in March 1982 after completing her current tour of duty. The ship was not to be replaced.

Despite the withdrawal from global commitment implicit in the defence review and its results, the United Kingdom still possessed a few overseas possessions and the scaling down of the Royal Navy now helped to convey the impression, right or wrong, that the United Kingdom had little further interest in them or their defence. Thus the way was opened for a revival of interest among other parties who had long coveted such far-flung remnants of empire as Belize and, more immediately, the Falkland Islands some 480 miles (770 km) to the north-east of Cape Horn at the southern extremity of the Americas. The Falkland Islands had never possessed any real economic value and now retained no strategic importance of the type that had made the islands important in World Wars I and II. (The same was not true of the Falkland Islands' dependencies of South Georgia and the South Sandwich group lying well

Seen here with three 500-lb (227-kg) Mk 82 bombs and two drop tanks, this A-4B was delivered straight from extensive maintenance to *Grupo 5* at Rio Gallegos, and was initially flown in an overall grey colour scheme. The serial number C-222 identifies this machine as one of the original 25 aircraft (C-201 to C-225) ordered by the FAA in 1966. An order for a further 25 A-4B warplanes (C-226 to C-250) was placed in 1970 and a final 25 A-4C warplanes (C-251 to C-275) were ordered in 1975

Seen at the combined airport and naval air base at Ushaia at the extreme south-eastern tip of Argentina on Tierra del Fuego, this was one of 16 F.27 twin-turboprop transports operated by the FAA. The first of these aircraft was delivered by Fokker in 1968, and the force comprised two Mk 400, 10 Mk 400M, two Mk 500 and two Mk 600 aircraft. The serial on the side of the rear fuselage identifies this machine as an F.27-400

off to the south-east, whose possession yielded the United Kingdom a legal access to Antarctica and its possibly enormous resources). Diplomatic negotiations, which had been undertaken from 1965, had led to an Argentine belief that the British would accede to Argentina's demands for sovereignty in the longer if not the shorter term. What the Argentines failed to take into any sort of account, however, was the fact that the 1,800 or so inhabitants of the Falkland Islands were determinedly opposed to any transfer of sovereignty from the United Kingdom to Argentina, and as a result the negotiations were entirely stalled.

Early in 1982, therefore, the junta (three-man army, navy and air force ruling body of Argentina) decided to react militarily to the problems occasioned by Argentine exasperation at the lack of progress at the negotiating table and the increasing pressure its rule was facing internally from forces wanting a return to democratic rule in Argentina. Aware of the fact that there were only vestigial British forces in the South Atlantic, and that these forces would soon dwindle to nothing, the junta decided that internal pressure could be relieved by an external adventure.

It seems probable that the junta originally planned to seize the Falkland Islands in the spring of the southern hemisphere, between June and October 1982, after the *Endurance* had left the region. However, plans were increasingly overtaken by events after Argentine scrap-metal workers, with a contract but without the required authority from the administration in the Falkland Islands, landed at Leith on South Georgia on 19 March from the Argentine fleet auxiliary *Bahia Buen Suceso* to start

Argentina's SH-3Ds participated in the original invasion. This one was used for clandestine operations and received an overall camouflage colour scheme

the work of dismantling and stripping the disused whaling station at that deserted settlement. The demolition workers raised the Argentine flag over Leith, and the *Endurance* (carrying 23 Royal Marines from the tiny garrison of the Falkland Islands) was despatched to investigate. On 23 March a small reconnaissance party was landed on the island, and the Royal Marines were put ashore on 31 March. In the way that seems inevitable in such circumstances, on 23 March the Argentine polar exploration vessel *Bahia Paraiso* was diverted from her ordinary duties to reinforce the Argentine party on South Georgia with Argentine marines, and the growing intensity of events persuaded Galtieri that matters could be further exploited to improve the survival chances of his junta by diverting Argentine attentions from domestic to international events, and on 23 March the decision was made to invade and occupy the Falkland Islands. As a first move, part of a major Argentine naval force was diverted from exercises in the north, off the coast of Uruguay, to undertake the invasion. The force allocated to Operation 'Rosario', as the undertaking was codenamed, departed two days later in two elements as Task Group 40 (invasion force) and Task Group 20 (covering force).

Although the increasing threat to the Falkland Islands was not yet fully evident to the British government, the heightening level of tension in the South Atlantic was reflected by the Conservative government's decision of 25 March to despatch nuclear-powered submarines to the region. By the end of March a clearer appreciation of the Argentines' intentions was becoming available, and it was decided on 31 March to start the assembly of a task force to undertake the recapture of the Falkland Islands if necessary. The task force was to comprise two main elements, namely Task Force 317 (surface vessels) and Task Force 324 (submarines).

The Argentine invasion of the Falkland Islands started at 04.30 hours (local time) on 2 April, when 150 marine commandos arrived by helicopter at Mullett Creek, a short distance to the south-west of Port Stanley, the capital of the Falkland Islands, and then moved overland to take the Royal Marine barracks, in fact empty, at Moody Brook west of the town. At 06.15 hours the main body of the Argentine force started to land at Yorke Bay to the east and the 68 Royal Marines of Naval Party 8901, which constituted the entire British garrison together with 12 sailors landed from the *Endurance,* were trapped by the approach of two Argentine forces. The Royal Marines fell back towards Government

With their sturdy landing gear and STOL field performance, all variants of the C-130 (here the first of Argentina's two KC-130H tankers) are capable of flying into and out of small airfields of indifferent quality, and this factor was notably important for the FAA, whose aircraft helped to maintain an air bridge between the mainland and BAM Malvinas until the closing stages of the Falklands war

House, delaying the invaders and killing at least two of them, but by 09.25 hours the governor of the islands, Rex Hunt, decided that with some 2,800 Argentine soldiers already ashore there was no virtue or military sense in continued resistance and surrendered. Later on the same day the first elements of the Argentine air force moved onto the islands with the arrival of FMA IA-58 Pucará light attack aircraft of *Grupo 3 de Ataque* and a Lockheed C-130 Hercules delivering a TPS-43F surveillance radar and its operating team.

One day later a very similar situation arose at Grytviken on South Georgia, which was held by the 23 Royal Marines landed by the *Endurance.* This party maintained its resistance for some two hours before surrendering, in the process killing four Argentines, destroying an Aérospatiale Puma helicopter of the Argentine army's *Batallón de Aviación de Combate 601,* and inflicting damage on a corvette.

The fact that the junta had miscalculated at the very beginning of the Argentine occupation of the Falkland Islands now started to become clear. Even as the Argentine authorities started to release photographs of the captured Royal Marines and emphasise the humiliating nature of this reverse for British arms, the first evidence started to appear that the junta had erred in its members' belief that the British would now acquiesce to the current situation and concede the Falkland Islands to Argentina. With speed and energy, the government of Margaret Thatcher began to deploy its considerable diplomatic skill and influence to begin the process

The Hercules turboprop-powered tanker was a vital link in the rapid movement of essential weapons and equipment from the United Kingdom to Ascension Island and then, after the aircraft had been fitted with an inflight-refuelling probe, to the ships of the task force at sea in the South Atlantic off the Falkland Islands

Fast long-range delivery of men and equipment to Ascension Island was the responsibility of the VC10 C.Mk 1 transports of the Royal Air Force's No. 10 Squadron

of isolating Argentina and securing a world-wide condemnation of the Argentine invasion. On 3 April the United Nations Security Council adopted Resolution 502 calling for a rapid Argentine evacuation of its forces from the Falkland Islands and demanding that the two sides look for a peaceful solution. Six days later the European Economic Community adopted a policy of trade sanctions against Argentina, and many other countries also did the same. Most importantly of all, by the end of the month the United States of America, after trying to hold itself aloof from a conflict between two allies and undertaking an attempt at neutral diplomatic mediation, decided to support the United Kingdom.

The British government and its supporters still hoped for a diplomatic solution but pressed ahead with military preparations. On 1 April seven Lockheed Hercules transport aircraft of the RAF delivered to Gibraltar essential supplies required by the Royal Navy, and also the air traffic control team and its equipment that would later be moved forward to Ascension Island, which was destined to become the mid-point focus of British air transport efforts between the United Kingdom and South Atlantic. Although Ascension Island is British-owned, its airfield was built by the Americans and operated by Pan American Airways as a base for the tracking of satellites: Wideawake Airfield, normally accustomed to

With her crew lining the flight deck, the light aircraft carrier HMS *Invincible* heads out into the English Channel as she departs the great naval base at Portsmouth on 5 April. One Sea Harrier FRS.Mk 1 warplane and four Sea King HAS.Mk 5 helicopters are visible on the forward and after ends of the flight deck

Troops disembark from a Sea King helicopter after arrival on board an aircraft carrier. Although intended primarily for the autonomous anti-submarine role, the Sea King was increasingly vital to the success of Operation 'Corporate' in the Falkland Islands campaign in the movement of men, equipment and supplies

some three aircraft movements per week, would soon be handling 400 movements per day.

On 2 April the British government decided to despatch a substantial task force to the South Atlantic. Had the junta adhered to its first plan and launched the invasion later in the year, this would have been a difficult if not impossible decision to make, for several major ships would have been withdrawn from service. The Argentine invasion found the aircraft carriers HMS *Invincible* and HMS *Hermes* and the assault ship HMS *Fearless* in British waters and therefore available for rapid despatch to the South Atlantic. The ships departed on 5 and 6 April together with four destroyers and seven frigates as well as six supply and four landing ship logistic (LSL) vessels of the Royal Fleet Auxiliary. They headed toward Ascension Island in the middle of the Atlantic where they were to link up with seven destroyers and frigates of the 1st Flotilla, withdrawn from Exercise 'Spring Train' in the Mediterranean. Air support was to be provided by 22 Sea Harrier V/STOL warplanes on the carriers. The task force began to come together under the command of Rear Admiral John T. 'Sandy' Woodward (who had sailed from Gibraltar on the destroyer HMS *Glamorgan* during 2 April) in the course of 7 April. On the same day the British revealed that a Maritime Exclusion Zone, some 200 nm (230 miles/370 km) in radius, would come into effect off the Falkland Islands five days later on the 12th. What was not revealed at the time was the fact that three nuclear-powered submarines, sent south as the crisis was beginning late in March, would also be in the theatre.

The major ships that departed Portsmouth and Devonport on the southern coast of England on 5 April comprised the aircraft carriers *Hermes* and *Invincible.* The former carried A Company of No. 42 Commando as well as fixed- and rotary-wing aircraft in the forms of the

Equipped with search radar, a magnetic anomaly detector with its sensor in the long tail 'sting' and an advanced system for the processing of acoustic data relayed from dropped sonobuoys, the Nimrod was well equipped to locate Argentine surface and sub-surface targets

Sea Harrier FRS.Mk 1 warplanes of the Fleet Air Arm's No. 800 Squadron supplemented by men and machines of the identically equipped No. 899 Squadron, the Westland Sea King HAS.Mk 5 anti-submarine helicopters of No. 826 Squadron and the Sea King HC.Mk 4 transport helicopters of No. 846 Squadron. The latter embarked the Sea Harrier FRS.Mk 1 warplanes of No. 801 Squadron again supplemented by machines and men of No. 899 Squadron, and the Sea King HAS.Mk 5 helicopters of No. 820 Squadron. The primary unit that departed on 6 April was the assault ship *Fearless* carrying some of the Sea King HC.Mk 4 helicopters of No. 846 Squadron. The requisitioned (STUFT, or Ship Taken Up From Trade) liner *Canberra* departed from Southampton on 9 April carrying some 2,000 men of Nos 40 and 42 Commandos and 3 Para. It was on 6 April that the RAF began to arrive on Ascension Island, where it joined the naval party already delivered by air, to create the initial establishment of the British Forces Support Unit Ascension Island: this first RAF element comprised two of No. 42 Squadron's BAe Nimrod MR.Mk 1 long-range maritime patrol and anti-submarine aircraft, which were entrusted with the provision of reconnaissance cover for the task force.

Considerably farther to the south, the Argentine forces had by this time located an information and control centre at Port Stanley, and the *Fuerza Aérea Argentina* (Argentine Air Force – FAA) had also instituted a new command structure to allow the creation of an integrated air operations capability: this *Teatro de Operaciones del Atlantico Sur* (South Atlantic Operational Theatre) had its headquarters at Comodoro Rivadavia.

COLOUR PLATES

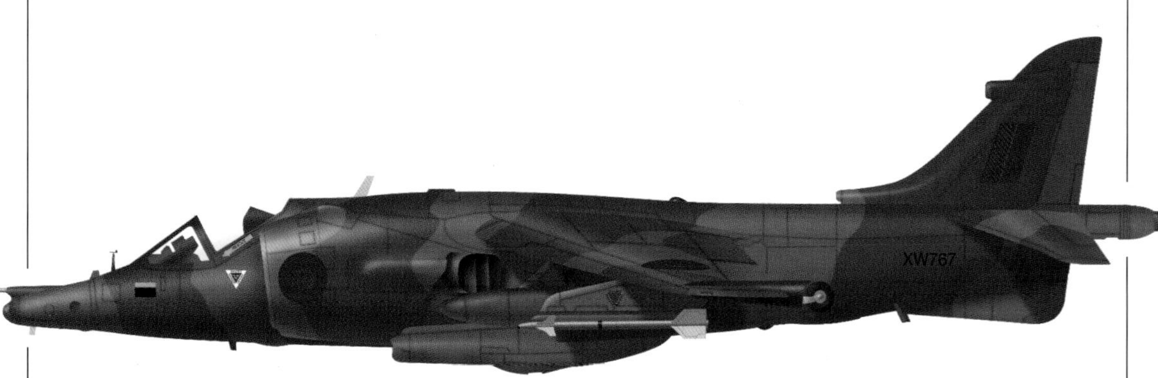

1
BAe Harrier GR.Mk 3, Serial Number: XW767, No. 1 Squadron, Royal Air Force, HMS *Hermes*

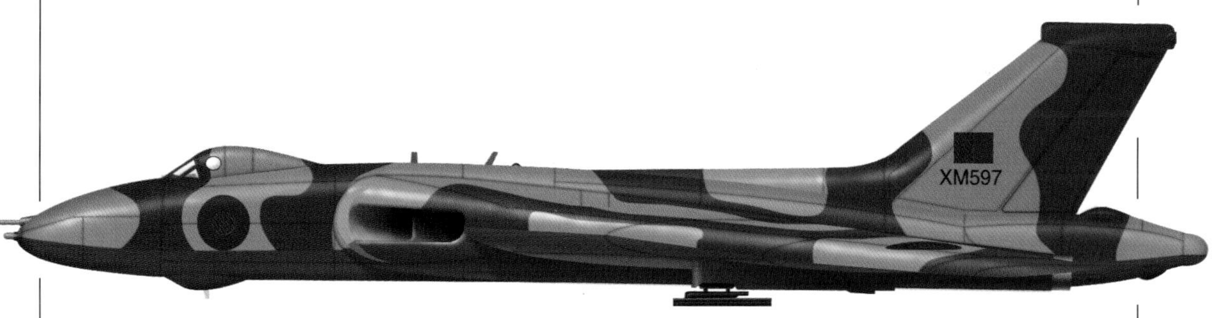

2
BAe Vulcan B.Mk 2A, Serial Number: XM597, No. 50 Squadron, Royal Air Force, Ascension Island

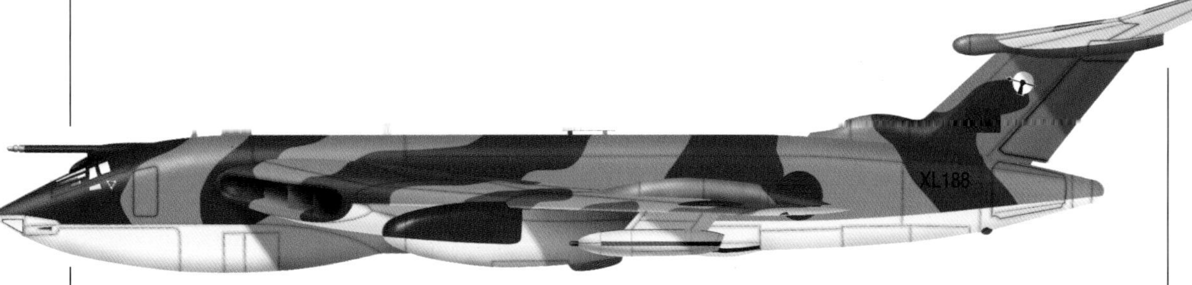

3
BAe Victor K.Mk 2, Serial Number: XL188, No. 55 Squadron, Royal Air Force, Ascension Island

4
BAe Sea Harrier FRS.Mk 1, Serial Number: ZA174, No. 801 Squadron, Fleet Air Arm, HMS *Invincible*

5
Boeing Chinook HC.Mk 1, Serial Number: ZA718, No. 18 Squadron, Royal Air Force

6
Aermacchi MB-339A, Serial Number: 4-A-113, 1 Escuadrilla de Ataque, Comando de la Aviación Naval Argentina

7
Dassault Super Etendard, Serial Number: 3-A-201, 2 Escuadrilla de Caza y Ataque, Comando de la Aviación Naval Argentina

8
McDonnell Douglas A-4Q Skyhawk, Serial Number: 3-A-304, 3 Escuadrilla de Caza y Ataque, Comando de la Aviación Naval Argentina

9
FMA IA-58A Pucará, Serial Number: A-549, Grupo 3 de Ataque, Fuerza Aérea Argentina

10
Dassault Mirage IIIEA, Serial Number: 1-007, Grupo 8 de Caza, Fuerza Aérea Argentina

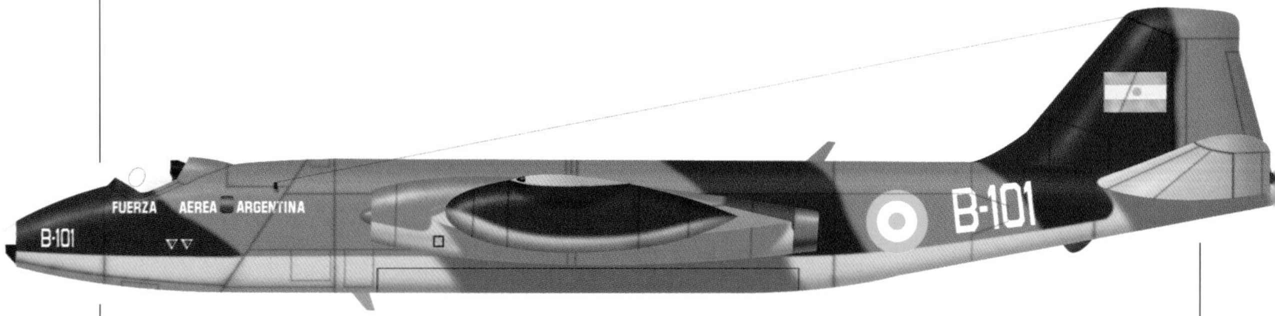

11
BAe Canberra B.Mk 62, Serial Number: B-101, Grupo 2 de Bombardeo, Fuerza Aérea Argentina

12
Grumman S-2E Tracker, Serial Number: 2-AS-26, Escuadrilla Anti-Submarina, Comando de la Aviación Naval Argentina

13
Learjet 35A, Serial Number: VR-17, I Escuadrón, Grupo Aérofotográfico, Fuerza Aérea Argentina

14
Lockheed L-188PF Electra, Serial Number: D730, 1 Escuadrilla de Sostén Logístico Móvil, Comando de la Aviación Naval Argentina

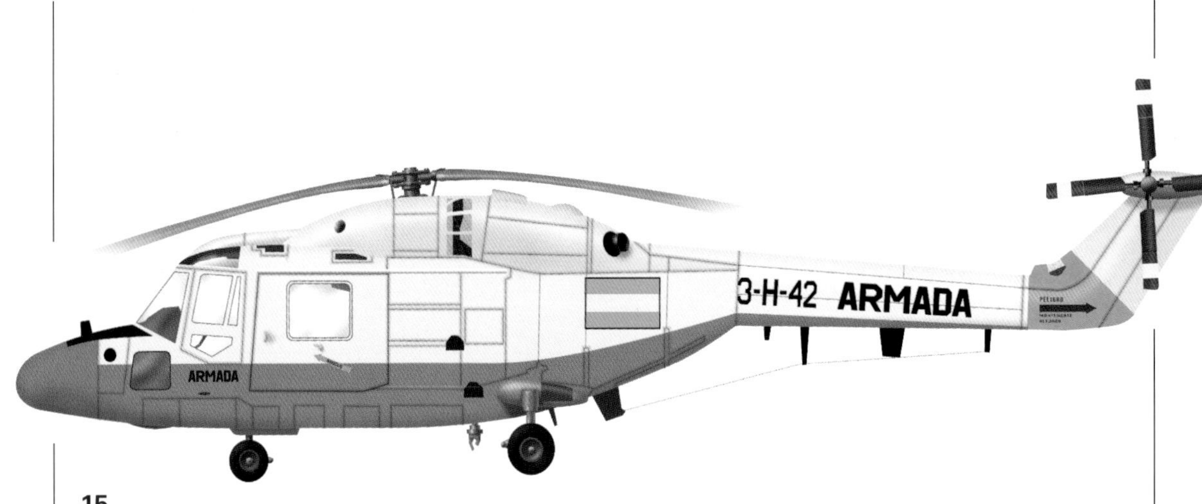

15
Westland Lynx Mk 23, Serial Number: 3-H-42, 1 Escuadrilla de Helicopteros, Comando de la Aviación Naval Argentina

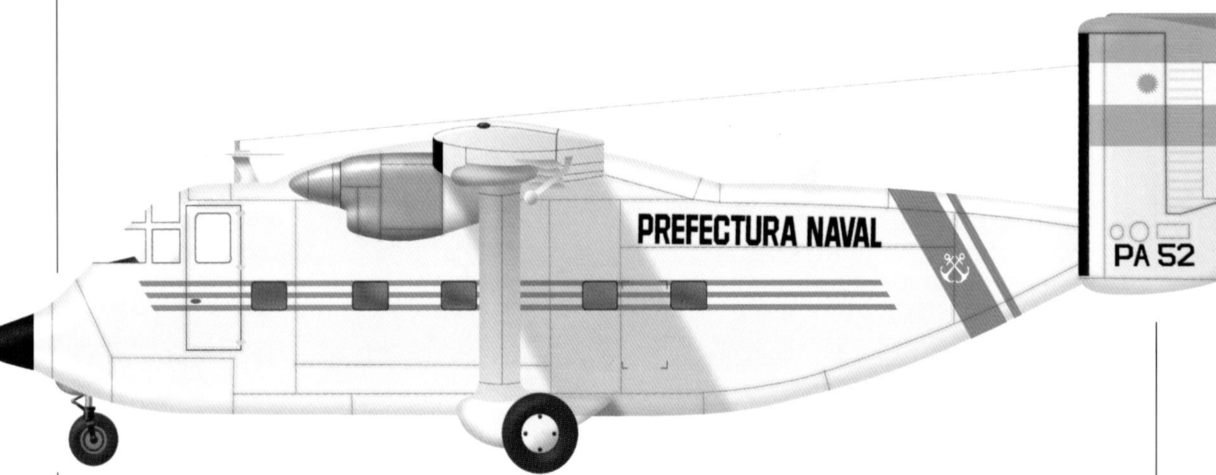

16
Shorts Skyvan 3M-400-7, Serial Number: PA-52, Prefectura Naval Argentina

1

2

3

4

5

ARMADA 3-A-205
MARINE 17
ARMADA 3-A-201
MARINE 44
ARMADA 3-A-204
ARMADA 3-A-202

6

7

8

9

10

11

12

13

14

15

16

17

18

19

THE TASK FORCE HEADS SOUTH

On or shortly after 10 April it is thought that BAe Canberra PR.Mk 9 reconnaissance aircraft of the RAF's No. 39 Squadron may have begun flying from the Punta Arenas air base in southern Chile after receiving the markings of the *Fuerza Aérea de Chile* in Belize while in transit from the United Kingdom, and it is also possible if not actually probable that BAe Nimrod R.Mk 1 electronic intelligence aircraft of the RAF's No. 51 Squadron also flew from Punta Arenas.

Ships from the forces that had steamed from Gibraltar and from British ports began to assemble off Ascension Island from 10 April, the date on which the cruise liner *Uganda* was requisitioned for rapid modification as a hospital ship. The pace of progress toward operations in the South Atlantic was now accelerating, as indicated in the repainting of aircraft in low-visibility colour schemes and the removal of many of their markings. For some of the task force's ships the pause at Ascension Island was very short. For example, the destroyer HMS *Antrim,* the frigate HMS *Plymouth* and the tanker RFA *Tidespring* embarked equipment and a small force of ground troops (M Company of No. 42 Commando, D Squadron of the Special Air Service (SAS), and a detachment of the Special Boat Squadron) plus helicopters: one Wessex HAS.Mk 3 machine of No. 737 Squadron on the *Antrim,* two Wessex HU.Mk 5 machines of No. 845 Squadron on the *Tidespring* and one Wasp HAS.Mk 1 machine of No. 829 Squadron on the *Plymouth.* These three ships were to steam south as Task Force 317.9 and join forces with the *Endurance* on 12 April for the implementation of Operation 'Paraquat', as the recapture of South Georgia was codenamed.

The Canberra PR.Mk 9 reconnaissance aircraft thought to have operated from the Chilean air base at Punta Arenas were machines of No. 59 Squadron equipped with a Texas Instruments infra-red linescan system

As these detached ships headed south, a major effort was being made off Ascension Island to rationalise the equipment and stores that had been rushed from the United Kingdom with little thought for correct combat loading factors. At the same time more equipment arrived by air from the United Kingdom and from the United States of America in the Hercules transports of the RAF's Lyneham Wing supplemented by the BAe VC10C.Mk 1 transports of No. 10 Squadron and also chartered civil aircraft. The task of rationalising the stores and equipment carried by

A Sea Harrier FRS.Mk 1 hovers over the bow of the container ship *Atlantic Conveyor,* on which an open-topped 'hangar' had been created for the storage and later erection of Wessex and Chinook helicopters by lining the sides of the deck with containers

the ships of the task force was entrusted largely to helicopters such as the Sea King anti-submarine machines of Nos 820 and 826 Squadrons, the Sea King assault transport machines of No. 846 Squadron, the Wessex transport machines of No. 845 Squadron, and the Wasp and Westland Lynx HAS.Mk 2 helicopters of the various ship's flights provided by Nos 815 and 829 Squadrons. These units and their hard-worked helicopters achieved miracles of reorganisation on the vital tasks of cross-decking equipment and supplies, and in the vertrep (vertical replenishment) of ships at sea.

The vertrep role continued even after the ships of the task force had departed from Ascension Island, and in the course of one such flight on the night of 23 April a Sea King HC.Mk 4 (ZA311) of No. 846 Squadron came down in the sea off the *Hermes* with the loss of one of its crew men.

As the ships of the task force pushed farther to the south, the threat of a pre-emptive strike by the Argentine navy, which included a number of capable conventional submarines, became more acute. As a result the RAF replaced the Nimrod MR.Mk 1 aircraft of No. 42 Squadron with more advanced Nimrod MR.Mk 2 aircraft provided by Nos 120, 201 and 206 Squadrons. As the ships of the task force were now entering what might be termed the Argentine theatre, far removed from the possibility of direct support by aircraft based at or staging through Ascension Island, long-range support capability was provided by the advent of the first BAe Victor K.Mk 2 inflight-refuelling tankers, some of which also possessed a useful capability for radar reconnaissance.

Argentine preparations for the continued occupation of the Falkland Islands and defence against any British effort to retake the islands meant

A Sea Harrier FRS.Mk 1 (foreground) and Harrier GR.Mk 3 are pictured over the aircraft carrier HMS *Hermes* in the South Atlantic

4-A-116 (0767) was the sixth of 10 MB-339A advanced trainer and light attack aircraft that the CANA ordered from Aermacchi in 1980 for delivery in 1981. The aircraft were operated by the 1 *Escuadrilla de Ataque*, but proved ineffective in the Falklands campaign

a steady development of the FAA's air strength in the theatre. On East Falkland the airfield at Port Stanley now became the *Base Aérea Militar* (BAM) Malvinas and BAM Condor was established at Goose Green farther to the south on the same island, and the *Comando de la Aviación Naval Argentina* (CANA), or Argentine naval air command, set up a base at Pebble Island off West Falkland as the *Estacion Aéronaval* (EA) Calderon.

As a result of this reorganisation and expansion, by a time late in April the FAA was able to deploy 24 FMA IA-58A Pucará light attack aircraft of *Grupo 3 de Ataque* C3A to BAM Malvinas and BAM Condor; and the CANA had located six Aermacchi MB-339A advanced trainer and light attack aircraft of the 1 *Escuadrilla de Ataque* at BAM Malvinas, and four

An Argentine Chinook being refuelled at Port Stanley. This aircraft was captured intact and later refurbished

Beech T-43C-1 armament trainer and light attack aircraft of the 3 *Escuadrilla de Ataque* at BAM Malvinas and EA Calderon. A limited search and rescue capability was provided by two Bell Model 212 light helicopters and two Boeing CH-47C medium helicopters of the FAA's *Grupo 7 de Coin Escuadron Helicopteros* from BAM Condor, with additional rescue and utility transport capacity generated by the *Comando de Aviación del Ejército* (Army Air Command) in the form of the diverse helicopters of the *Battalón de Aviación de Combate* 601 unit at Moody Brook and the *Prefectura Naval Argentina* (Argentine Naval Agency, or coast guard) in the form of two Shorts Skyvan aircraft and one Aérospatiale Puma helicopter based at BAM Malvinas.

BAM Malvinas and, to a lesser extent, BAM Condor, which were the two main centres of Argentine air strength in the Falkland Islands, saw a steady stream of transport aircraft bringing in more men, equipment and supplies, and were protected from air attack by 35-mm and 30-mm anti-aircraft guns as well as Shorts Tigercat and Euromissile Roland surface-to-air missiles, all manned by FAA officer cadets specially allocated to the airfield defence role.

This was not the full extent of the Argentine commitment of air power to the protection of its position in the Falkland Islands, which lay within notional range of warplanes operating from several air bases located in the southern part of the Argentine mainland. These bases were the *Base Aérea Naval* (BAN) Almirante Zar (eight Canberra B.Mk 62 bombers of the *Grupo 2 de Bombardeo*); BAM Comodoro Rivadavia (several Dassault Mirage IIIEA supersonic fighters of the *Grupo 8 de Caza* and eight IA-58A

Carrying a centreline bomb and two drop tanks, this A-4C of *Grupo 4* awaits the start of a mission from the base at San Julian

Ground crew cheer off an A-4B Skyhawk of *Grupo 5* as it accelerates along the runway at Rio Gallegos before lifting off on a mission

attack aircraft of the *Grupo 4 de Ataque*); San Julian (10 IAI Dagger supersonic fighters of the II/ *Grupo 6 de Caza* and 15 McDonnell Douglas A-4C Skyhawk attack aircraft of the *Grupo 4 de Caza*); BAM Rio Gallegos (26 A-4B attack aircraft of the *Grupo 5 de Caza* and 10 Mirage IIIEA supersonic fighters of the *Grupo 8 de Caza*); and BAN Rio Grande (with 10 Dagger supersonic fighters of the III/ *Grupo 6 de Caza,* 5 Dassault Super Etendard maritime attack aircraft of the 2 *Escuadrilla de Caza y Ataque,* and eight A-4Q attack aircraft of the 3 *Escuadrilla de Caza y Ataque*).

There were also a number of aircraft held in reserve, but in overall terms the FAA could call on some 110 operational aircraft including the short-range Pucará machines based on the mainland, while the CANA had a land-based strength of just 12 operational aircraft as one of the five Super Etendard machines was being cannibalised for spares since the delivery of further Super Etendard aircraft and all spares for earlier French-supplied aircraft had been halted as a result of the sanctions imposed by the EEC in response to British requests.

As always, accurate and timely reconnaissance was essential to the planning of any operation that was to gain a reasonable level of success, and in preparation for Operation 'Paraquat' three long-range radar sorties were flown by Victor aircraft. The first of these, undertaken during the night of 20/21 April by a Victor K.Mk 2 of No. 57 Squadron, required the support of eight tanker sorties in the course of a flight of more than 7,000 miles (11,275 km) in 14 hours 45 minutes for reconnaissance of an

The Dagger was first committed to the Falklands war in its fighter form. C-401 was the first Dagger delivered from Israel, and is seen here at San Julian with Shafrir 2 air-to-air missiles. Clearly inspired by the AIM-9 Sidewinder, the Shafrir series had a larger-diameter body but an engagement envelope of only limited aspect

area of 150 sq miles (388.5 km).

The three reconnaissance flights provided useful information and thus helped significantly in the finalisation of the plans for the assault on South Georgia. The first step in Operation 'Paraquat' was the insertion of an SAS party on Fortuna Glacier, a task achieved on 21 April by the Wessex HAS.Mk 3 of No. 737 Squadron and two Wessex HU.Mk 5 machines of No. 845 Squadron. However, soon after the insertion, the weather rapidly turned so appalling that the SAS party radioed for an evacuation during the following morning. While attempting to lift out the SAS troopers, two Wessex HU.Mk 5 helicopters crashed while trying to land in white-out conditions, none on board suffering serious injury, so the SAS troopers and the crews of the lost helicopters were pulled back to safety by the other Wessex.

A Westland Lynx Mk 2 helicopter prepares to land on the 'Type 42' class destroyer HMS *Birmingham* during the Lynx's qualification trials in 1977. Used only in modest numbers during the Falklands war, the Lynx proved itself a capable and reliable helicopter, but the *Birmingham* was not deployed to the South Atlantic

Two days later the British sighted the decidedly elderly Argentine submarine ARA *Santa Fe* off South Georgia, and the frigate HMS *Brilliant,* carrying two Lynx HAS.Mk 2 helicopters, arrived to supplement TF.317.9. The first real contact with the *Santa Fe* was made by the *Antrim,* whose Wessex helicopter tried to depth-charge the Argentine submarine. The attack damaged the submarine, whose captain decided to return to Grytviken. As the *Santa Fe* was heading back to South Georgia it was unsuccessfully attacked by a torpedo from one of the *Brilliant's* Lynx helicopters, and then by AS.12 wire-guided light air-to-surface missiles from the Wasp helicopters of the *Plymouth* and the *Endurance.* Severely damaged, the submarine gained Grytviken and was beached alongside the jetty.

The British now decided that the evident lack of Argentine strength

A Wasp HAS.Mk 1 helicopter from the ice patrol ship HMS *Endurance* is captured by the camera over Grytviken on South Georgia Island some time later in April. Evident just at the surface of the water is the sail of the beached Argentine submarine *Santa Fe*

and resolution on South Georgia made it feasible to extemporise an assault at short notice. This effectively ruled out the use of the Royal Marines on the *Tidespring,* which was some 200 miles (320 km) to the north. In preparation for the operation a naval gunfire support officer was delivered by helicopter to his spotting position and 30 troopers of the SAS landed on the coast. Soon after this 235 rounds of naval gunfire rained down on and round the Argentine positions as additional troopers were landed from the *Plymouth* and the *Endurance.* Dispirited and realising the hopeless nature of its position, the Argentine garrison of Grytviken surrendered without putting up any sort of resistance, and Leith's small Argentine garrison followed suit during the following day.

Meanwhile the task force had steamed from Ascension Island on and shortly after 18 April, and in the United Kingdom a follow-on force of ground troops had started training in the Brecon Beacons, the area thought most similar in geography and climate to those of the Falkland Islands. This force was the 5th Infantry Brigade (2nd Scots Guards, 1st Welsh Guards and 7th Gurkha Rifles), and was scheduled to depart from the United Kingdom during the first part of May.

As it headed south on 21 April, the task force was sighted by a Boeing Model 707 transport operated in the reconnaissance role by the FAA. The Argentine aeroplane was intercepted and shepherded away rather than attacked by a Sea Harrier of No. 800 Squadron. Six days later the task force had arrived in a position to the north-east of the Falkland Islands, and on 29 April the growing threat of British interception persuaded the FAA to end its daylight transport flights into the islands. On the following day the international isolation of Argentina became one step more acute when the United States of America ended its attempts to mediate diplomatically and formally sided with British.

There were now some 70 British ships in the waters off the Falklands, and the Maritime Exclusion Zone now became the Total Exclusion Zone. The possibility of a further increase in the air strength available to the task force had been created by the creation of No. 809 Squadron at the Royal Naval Air Station Yeovilton in Somerset out of development and reserve aircraft. The first six Sea Harrier warplanes of this unit flew out to Ascension Island via Banjul in West Africa, each of the aircraft undertaking no fewer than 14 inflight refuellings in the course of this lengthy self-deployment, and then embarked on the large transport *Atlantic Conveyor* on 5 May. By this date the Sea Harrier warplanes of Nos 800 and 801

With a flight-ready Sea Harrier FRS.Mk 1 at the forward end of its deck, the *Atlantic Conveyor* heads south as work begins on the assembly of aircraft for subsequent delivery flights to their parent ships. Between the two 'walls' of containers are 11 Harrier GR.Mk 1 close support and Sea Harrier FRS.Mk 1 multi-role fighter warplanes, four Wessex helicopters including two in the process of assembly, and at the extreme forward end of the port-side row the sole Chinook HC.Mk 1 to be assembled and flown off the ship before she was sunk

The Vulcan B.Mk 2 was in the final stages of its withdrawal from service, but sufficient aircraft of this type were provided by three squadrons (including No. 101 Squadron, to which this machine belonged in the happier times of 1976) to make possible the series of 'Black Buck' long-range missions intended to render BAM Malvinas (Stanley Airport) unusable by the Argentines

Squadrons were operating regular Combat Air Patrols (CAPs) over the task force as the final preparations were made for offensive operations against the Argentine garrison of the Falkland Islands and any support that might be directed from the Argentine mainland.

The Falklands war may be said to have started fully on 1 May, when a Vulcan B.Mk 2 of No. 101 Squadron made the first 'Black Buck' bombing raid from Wideawake airfield on Ascension Island. This raid lasted 14 hours 50 minutes in all, and demanded 15 Victor K.Mk 2

Other damage was caused by the first 'Black Buck' mission on 1 May, some of the 20 1,000-lb (454-kg) bombs that did not hit the runway cratering the airfield, damaging installations and incapacitating a number of aircraft such as the IA-58A Pucará in the foreground

A Harrier of No. 1 Squadron leaves the 'ski jump' on the forward end of HMS *Hermes'* flight deck. The warplane is carrying two AIM-9L Sidewinder air-to-air missiles and two 1,000-lb (454-kg) bombs. More use of the Harrier force could have been made in the early stages of the land campaign if the *Hermes* had not been held so far to the east for fear of Argentine air attack

sorties and no fewer than 18 inflight refuellings to get the single Vulcan bomber over its target, where the full load of 21 1,000-lb (454-kg) bombs was dropped from an altitude of 10,000 ft (3,050 m) across the runway of Port Stanley airfield. The bombs were dropped diagonally across the runway in an effort to ensure that at least one bomb hit the primary target, but in the event it was only one bomb that did hit the runway, causing only relatively minor cratering damage. The detonation of other bombs damaged both aircraft and installations.

In an effort to capitalise on what was hoped would be considerable Argentine confusion after the Vulcan's attack, the *Hermes* launched 12 Sea Harrier warplanes of No. 800 Squadron from 07.48 hours to attack the airfields at Port Stanley and Goose Green. In a somewhat complex undertaking, nine of the Sea Harrier warplanes bombed Port Stanley from three directions using a combination of toss bombing and conventional bombing for the delivery of 1,000-lb (454-kg) bombs fitted with impact and delay-action fuses as well as BL755 cluster bombs. The raid achieved little in the way of decisive damage, but the airfield was rendered unsafe for Argentine operations for some time. The other three Sea Harrier warplanes undertook a generally more successful attack on Goose Green, in the process rendering three Pucará warplanes out of commission for the duration of the war and killing one Argentine pilot as he prepared to take off.

Later in the same morning the destroyer HMS *Glamorgan* and the frigates HMS *Alacrity* and HMS *Arrow* undertook a gun bombardment of Argentine positions in Port Stanley, and British armed helicopters were also in action over various parts of the Falkland Islands. There are suggestions that the scale of the British air and naval operations on this day persuaded the Argentines that an assault landing was imminent, and from a time early in the afternoon the FAA flew several missions against British warships but found few targets. The Mirage IIIEA and Dagger fighters of *Grupos 8* and *6 de Caza* provided cover for eight A-4 attack warplanes of *Grupos 4* and *5* and the Canberra bombers of *Grupo 2 de Bombardeo.*

Both the pilots and their ground crews were happy with the simplicity and thus the reliability of the Skyhawk light attack warplane. This factor was particularly important when the aircraft, such as these A-4B machines of *Grupo 5,* were deployed to austerely equipped air bases in the inhospitable south of Argentina

Armed with a single R530E air-to-air missile and carrying two drop tanks, this Mirage IIIEA is being prepared for a sortie from the decidedly austerely equipped airfield at Rio Gallegos

Later in the same day *Grupo 8* lost two of its Mirage IIIEA fighters to AIM-9L short-range air-to-air missiles launched by the Sea Harrier fighters of No. 801 Squadron, but a small number of Dagger fighters attacked the ships bombarding Stanley and inflicted a small measure of damage. A Dagger from a separate flight was destroyed by a Sea Harrier of No. 800 Squadron, and No. 801 Squadron scored its third success with the destruction of a Canberra B.Mk 62 some 150 miles (240 km) to the north-west of Port Stanley. The Sea Harrier force had enjoyed a profitable day without a single loss, and in the process had proved that the combination of the subsonic Sea Harrier and the Sidewinder missile was superior to the supersonic Mirage/Dagger series with cannon armament.

DOMINANCE OF THE SEA HARRIER

A closer look at the three occasions on which Sea Harrier fighters bested Argentine fighters in the course of 1 May reveals how the combination of the Sea Harrier fighter and Sidewinder missile, when flown by better trained and tactically more astute British pilots, prevailed over the notionally superior fighters of the FAA.

Early in the afternoon of 1 May, Flight Lieutenant Paul Barton, on detachment from the RAF to the Fleet Air Arm, was piloting one of two Sea Harrier FRS.Mk 1 fighters of No. 801 Squadron which were providing a combat air patrol to the west of the task force when the approach of an incoming force of Argentine warplanes was reported from the *Invincible's* command centre. The report indicated a pair of aircraft some 120 miles (193 km) to the west, with two more aircraft some 15 miles (24 km) behind them and a further two farther to the rear. Faced with odds of possibly six-to-two, Barton and his wing man, Lieutenant Commander John Eyton-Jones, were glad that further Sea Harrier fighters were closing to provide a welcome boost in the British strength.

Carrying drop tanks and AIM-9 Sidewinder short-range air-to-air missiles, this Sea Harrier FRS.Mk 1 is just leaving the flight deck of the light aircraft carrier HMS *Invincible*

Even so, in the short term the two British fighters faced the prospect of action against two and possibly six Argentine warplanes, probably Mirage IIIEA supersonic fighters. The two British pilots were confident that the subsonic Sea Harrier with its modern systems and weapons was superior, especially in any sort of turning engagement, to the supersonic Mirage IIIEA with its older systems and weapons. What the British fighter pilots feared was that the Argentine pilots would use their fighters to best effect by avoiding any type of turning engagement, in which the Mirage IIIEA's energy would soon bleed off as a result of its large delta wing, and instead opt for a series of slashing attacks from different directions to bracket the British fighters and also ensure that their own aircraft lost minimum energy.

The FAA ordered a total of 17 Mirage IIIEA fighters from Dassault. The first batch of 10 aircraft was ordered in 1970, together with two Mirage IIIDA two-seaters, and seven more machines were ordered in 1977. As seen here on two aircraft of *Grupo 8,* the machines of the second batch were each equipped for the underwing carriage of two R550 Magic short-range air-to-air missiles. In the background is an A-4B Skyhawk of *Grupo 5*

The two Sea Harrier fighters were flying at 15,000 ft (4,570 m), and decided to remain at that altitude as the thicker air of this altitude would adversely affect the performance of the Mirage IIIEA machines, reducing their maximum speed and adversely affecting their fuel consumption. Here the two British pilots were clearly seeking to exploit the old adage that success in air combat goes to the man who successfully seeks to tackle his opponent in the blend of speed, altitude and manoeuvring which exploits the advantages of his own aeroplane while denying his opponent the opportunity for full exploitation of his own aeroplane's advantages: it was readily apparent that that the Sea Harrier was at its best vis-à-vis the Mirage IIIEA in a low/medium-altitude arena and a short-range turning engagement.

On the other side of the coin, of course, the Argentine fighters were cruising at 34,450 ft (10,500 m), and their pilots were reluctant to lose the advantages of greater altitude and higher speed. The task of the Argentine pilots was now to lure the Sea Harriers to the higher altitude in which the Argentines' French-built fighters would be able to use their own advantages. For several minutes, therefore, the two forces manoeuvred defensively, each out of range of the other's missiles, but then a shortage of fuel dictated that the Argentine fighters break away and turn west toward the Argentine mainland. The Sea Harriers returned to their carrier to refuel and await another opportunity.

In the following hours several similar encounters were recorded as the pilots of the opposing forces searched for any weakness in the others' tactical thinking. Early in the afternoon Sea Harrier fighters of No. 801 Squadron had their first brush with the enemy when they intercepted a flight of three T-34C-1 light attack aircraft of the CANA's 4 *Escuadrilla de Ataque.* These turboprop-powered aircraft, which were in essence trainers with a light armament capability, were planning to strafe British warships undertaking a naval gunfire attack on BAM Malvinas at Port Stanley when the Sea Harriers of Lieutenant Commander 'Sharkey' Ward and Lieutenant Mike Watson were vectored onto them and lost

This Mirage IIIEA of *Grupo 8* is taking off on a combat air patrol with a single R530E medium-range air-to-air missile. Using semi-active radar guidance, this weapon proved far less capable than the IR-homing and therefore fully autonomous AIM-9 Sidewinder used by the British, and only one such missile was fired during the Falklands war, achieving no success as no adequate radar lock had been secured before missile launch

height through the cloud cover. As one of the British pilots later recalled, 'We were about 25 miles north of Port Stanley. We turned south, started to descend and picked up the contacts on radar close to the coast. As we came out of the bottom of the cloud we saw them, about a mile away. They saw us at about the same time. We turned in towards them, I saw they were T-34s and took a long range shot at them with my guns. They went straight up into cloud, I went after them. In the cloud I very nearly hit one. I just missed his right wing as I came past him, very close.'

The British pilots immediately dropped down under the cloud cover in tight turns just in time to watch as the Argentine aircraft headed into the region protected by the anti-aircraft defences of BAM Malvinas. Returning to medium altitude once more to resume their patrol, the two British pilots were soon involved in another stand-off 'non-engagement' with Argentine fighters at higher altitude. As the two forces sparred with each other, Ward realised that there appeared to be three condensation trails approaching the area, and hoped that at last this presaged an Argentine descent to lower altitude. Ward later said that 'I tried to lock one of my missiles on one of them, but the "contrails" turned out to be smoke trails from missiles they had fired at us! They must have fired from well out of range, because the nearest missile went past me by a long way and fell into the sea.' It was now clear that the Argentine pilots had hoped for a hit by firing missiles at extreme range without a proper lock on any target.

In the closing stages of the afternoon, the FAA launched a force of about 20 fighter, fighter-bomber and bomber warplanes to undertake a co-ordinated attack on the ships of the British task force. First to reach the region in which the ships of the task force were operating were the Mirage IIIEA fighters, and here they encountered a combat air patrol of Sea Harriers, one of them flown by Barton on his third sortie of the day. For a short time there followed the type of hesitant manoeuvring that had characterised earlier encounters, but then two Mirage IIIEA fighters descended to medium altitude to try a more decisive approach. Warned by the command centre of the destroyer *Glamorgan,* whose radar was providing the data for the ship's control officer, the British pilots, with Barton leading and Lieutenant Steve Thomas as his wing man, turned their aircraft toward the Argentine thrust. The two Sea Harrier fighters were flying at 11,000 ft (3,355 m) in the standard tactical disposition for a defensive engagement: line abreast with the aircraft about 1 mile (1.6 km) distant from each other so that each pilot could cover the blind zone behind and below his partner's aeroplane.

The Argentine aircraft were machines of the *Grupo 8 de Caza,* the FAA's only dedicated interceptor unit, and were flown by Captain Garcia Cuerva with Lieutenant Carlos Perona as his wing man. Thomas was the

The scene on part of HMS *Invincible's* flight deck as the ship takes on stores from a supply vessel alongside. Although lightweight anti-submarine torpedoes (right) were carried by the helicopters providing the ships of the task force with protection against the possible threat of Argentine submarine attack, the most important weapon employed in the early phases of the campaign was the AIM-9L version of the Sidewinder air-to-air missile (left), of which the Sea Harrier FRS.Mk 1 carried two under its wing

first to secure radar contact with the incoming Argentine aircraft, and thus took over the lead. As Thomas subsequently related, 'We were running in towards each other, head-on. I was doing about 400 knots, Paul accelerated to about 550 knots and pulled away to the right, to try and get around the back of them. I locked my radar on to their leader, then I began looking for the others – I couldn't believe that a pair of fighters would come in alone like that. Their formation was poor, what the Americans call "welded wing", flying very close together.' Looking for flying of a greater tactical acuity from their opponents, Thomas and Barton felt that the only reason for the Argentine pilots to do this was to draw in the British fighters and so facilitate the arrival of another pair of Mirage IIIEA fighters to catch the Sea Harrier machines in a pincer attack.

Thomas and Barton could not detect more Argentine fighters, however, and therefore closed on the two Argentine aircraft from two angles. Barton manoeuvred into position to take the Argentine fighters in the flank: 'My job now was to act as "shooter", to get behind the bogeys and attack them if they were identified as hostile. I accelerated to maximum speed and eased right to get displacement, locking my radar on to the No. 2 as I did so. I dived down, visually acquiring the bogeys at about five miles. I was relieved to see them visually – the eye is much better at comprehending three-dimensional information and I didn't really look at the radar again. I was using 110 per cent concentration for the attack. The leader came across my track from right to left at about 2½ miles and as he did so began a very gentle port turn.' Barton increased his banked turn and kept inside the two Argentine warplanes, and then realised that the Argentine wing man would cross in front of him at about maximum cannon range. The British pilot loosed a burst from his two 30-mm weapons, but saw no evidence of either any hits or indeed that the Argentine pilots had even spotted him.

At this stage the pair of Argentine fighters were close to Thomas, who later told of the events in the following words: 'I got a visual at about eight miles and saw it was a Mirage. And I could also see his No. 2, just to the right and behind. I was trying to lock a Sidewinder on to him but the missile would not acquire, I didn't get any growl so I couldn't fire it. At five miles their leader launched a missile at me, but I saw it diverge and go down to my left. At the same time something came off the second aircraft; it was tumbling, obviously a missile that had misfired. I didn't feel threatened by either missile.'

With the two sides closing at a speed of some 1,000 mph (1,600 km/h), Thomas now pulled pack on his stick to ensure that his Sea Harrier passed above the Mirage IIIEA aircraft, and then rolled into a starboard turn as the Argentine aircraft passed below him in a gentle port turn, still without spotting Barton's Sea Harrier, which was closing on the fighter flown by Perona. Barton recalled that 'I held the turn, still keeping him [Perona] and his leader in view through the top of my canopy. As I continued into his six the 'winder began to growl as it got its lock angle. This was a welcome noise because it confirmed my chance to get him and he was now outside gun range and separating fast. I completed the turn and was on his tail at about 500 yards. I was doing about 350 kt, but he was going about 150 kt faster and began to pull away. I was aware that he was faster than I was but with the 'winder locked up and well within range I was confident of getting him.'

Barton pushed the nose down slightly to get below the Mirage IIIEA, which would thus be seen against the cold of the sky and so help ensure that the Sidewinder missile's seeker secured the best possible lock on its target, and then fired the weapon on the launcher under the starboard wing. 'At first I thought it had failed. It came off the rail and ducked down. I had not fired a 'winder before so its behaviour at launch was new to me. I was surprised not to see it home straight in - to see it duck down was disconcerting. I'd begun to wonder if it was a dud. It took about half a mile for it to get its trajectory sorted out, then it picked itself up and for the last half mile it just homed straight in. The missile flight time was about four seconds, then the Mirage exploded in a brilliant blue, orange and red fireball.'

Barton was sure that the pilot could not have escaped the destruction of the Mirage, but in fact Perona ejected and was recovered by Argentine forces.

Meanwhile Thomas was pressing on with his attack on Garcia Cuerva: 'I was continuing my turn and the enemy leader was doing quite a hard descending turn to the left, going down very fast towards the top of the solid cloud cover at 4,000 ft. I'm not sure if he knew where I was. I rolled into a vertical descent behind him, locked on one of my missiles and fired it. The missile streaked after him and just before he reached cloud I saw it pass close to his tail. Then both the aircraft and the missile vanished.'

Three Dagger warplanes of *Grupo 6* are seen with drop tanks ready for take-off at San Julian

The Sea Harriers were now running short of fuel and broke away to return to the *Invincible,* when Barton was accorded a 'confirmed' victory and Thomas with a 'probable' victory. It was only after the end of the war that it was revealed that Thomas should also be credited with a 'confirmed' victory. Triggered by its proximity fuse, the warhead of the Sidewinder fired by Thomas exploded beside the Argentine warplane and caused significant damage. Losing fuel rapidly from his machine's ruptured tanks, Cuerva tried to reach BAM Malvinas for an emergency landing. However, as he neared the airfield, Cuerva released his drop tanks and Argentine gunners, believing that these were bombs, opened fire and destroyed the Mirage IIIEA, in the process killing Cuerva.

The Sea Harrier had achieved its first 'kills', and more followed without significant delay as only minutes later two aircraft of No. 800 Squadron came under attack from Dagger warplanes of the *Grupo 6 de Caza.* As the Sea Harrier warplanes flown by Lieutenant Martin Hale and Flight Lieutenant Tony Penfold tried to get themselves into a firing position, one of the Dagger fighters fired a missile at the aeroplane of Hale, who dived away steeply in an effort to break the missile's lock. Even so, the missile followed the Sea Harrier for some distance before failing. Climbing to rejoin the action, Hale saw Penfold down the other Dagger with a Sidewinder shot that detonated close to its target. The Dagger was mortally wounded and, losing parts of its airframe, dived into the sea.

Only a few more minutes separated Penfold's success from the next Sea Harrier engagement, when a pair of the British fighters, flown by Lieutenant Commander Mike Broadwater and Lieutenant Al Curtiss of No. 801 Squadron, encountered three Canberra B.Mk 62 bombers of the *Grupo 2 de Bombardeo* en route to attack the ships of the British task force. Curtiss destroyed one of the bombers with a Sidewinder missile and the remaining pair of aircraft turned back. Broadwater launched both his Sidewinder missiles at the bombers as they headed back to the Argentine mainland, but neither missile scored.

The first day of air combat in the Falklands war had ended in decisive

The Harrier GR.Mk 3 was generally not equipped for the carriage of air-to-air missiles, but the aircraft of No. 1 Squadron deployed to the Falkland Islands were adapted for the carriage of two Sidewinder missiles for improved self-defence capability. In addition to two Sidewinder and two drop tanks under its wing, this Harrier also carries two 30-mm Aden fixed forward-firing cannon in a side-by-side pair of conformal pods under the fuselage between the two units of the main landing gear

British victory, for without loss the Sea Harriers of Nos 800 and 801 Squadrons had encompassed the destruction of two Mirage, one Dagger and one Canberra warplanes. The British pilots were well satisfied with their performance and that of their aircraft, but were also realistic enough to realise that the Argentine pilots would digest the implications of the day's activities and return with improved tactics. Good as the Sea Harrier clearly was, its pilots were too professional to think that the two squadrons would continue to operate without loss to the Mirage IIIEA fighters flown by Argentina's premier fighter unit. What the British pilots did not know, however, was that the 'Black Buck 1' raid, which had attacked BAM Malvinas before dawn on 1 May, was leading to a revision in the Argentine disposition. The FAA, now fearing that Vulcan bombers could strike at strategic targets on the Argentine mainland, had decided to reserve the Mirage IIIEA fighters of the *Grupo 8 de Caza* for defence of mainland bases. So, with the exception of an few more sorties over the Falkland Islands, where they carefully avoided any Sea Harrier fighters, the Mirage IIIEA force spent the rest of the war at readiness on airfields that could have been threatened but were in fact never attacked. Moreover, from this day forward the Dagger was employed as a fighter-bomber rather than pure fighter, and for the rest of the war did not operate over the Falkland Islands with air-to-air missiles. Thus in the remaining six weeks of the war British pilots were faced by many forms of danger, but not missile-armed Argentine fighters.

Pilots and deck crew prepare one of the A-4Q warplanes of 3 *Escuadrilla* on ARA *Veinticinco de Mayo* for the mission that was planned for 1 May against the ships of the British task force but not in fact flown

This was not the full extent of the day's air activities, moreover, for the helicopters of the task force had also been busy. One of the most notable events was a sortie of no less than 10 hours 20 minutes by a Sea King HAS.Mk 5, a machine of No. 826 Squadron which had lifted off with two complete crews to search for the Argentine submarine *San Luis* and had refuelled in flight twice, from the frigates *Brilliant* and *Yarmouth.*

On 2 May, Sea King HC.Mk 4 helicopters of No. 846 Squadron delivered troopers of the SAS's G Squadron on the Falkland Islands during the early morning at the start of an extended ground reconnaissance effort. The same day also saw the sinking of the obsolescent Argentine cruiser *General Belgrano,* which was torpedoed by the nuclear-powered attack submarine HMS *Conqueror* and sank with the

The Sea King HC.Mk 4 is the Royal Navy's counterpart of the Commando, the land-based development of the Sea King for the export market, and is used for support of the Royal Marines. This machine is pictured while lifting a 105-mm (4.13-in) L118A1 Light Gun for delivery to the troops on East Falkland

A Sea Harrier hovers above the extemporised flight deck over the forward part of the Cunard line's container ship *Atlantic Conveyor.* The ship was sunk by an Exocet missile on 25 May, having flown off her load of vital Harrier warplanes to the aircraft carriers one week earlier, but went down with a mass of equipment including 10 Wessex and three Chinook helicopters – the one fortunate fact for the British was that one other Chinook had taken off from the ship just before the attack and was therefore saved to become the sole heavy-lift helicopter available for the land campaign on East Falkland

loss of many men as well as its Aérospatiale Alouette III helicopter. The Argentine navy also suffered the loss of another helicopter when a Lynx Mk 23 anti-submarine machine hit the destroyer *Santisima Trinidad.*

Early on the morning of 3 May, the Lynx HAS.Mk 2 helicopters of the destroyers HMS *Glasgow* and HMS *Coventry* used their Sea Skua lightweight anti-ship missiles to damage the Argentine patrol vessel *Alferez Sobel,* which had been searching for the crew of the Canberra downed by No. 801 Squadron.The *Alferez Sobel* had originally been located by a Sea King helicopter of No. 826 Squadron. On the same day the Argentines lost two aircraft. An Aermacchi MB-339A of the 1 *Escuadrilla de Ataque* crashed on approach to BAM Malvinas, and a Skyvan transport was lost to naval gunfire.

With an amphibious landing and subsequent land campaign now increasingly likely, it was important that the ground forces should be provided with a greater weight of ground-attack capability than could be provided by the Fleet Air Arm's Sea Harrier force, which would still have to provide cover against the possibility of Argentine air attack. On 4 May, therefore, the first Harrier GR.Mk 3 ground-attack and close support warplane of the RAF's No. 1 Squadron lifted off from St Mawgan in Cornwall and made a non-stop flight of 9 hours 15 minutes to reach Wideawake Airfield on Ascension Island after a flight of some 4,600 miles (7,400 km). More Harrier warplanes covered the same route over the next couple of days, and on 6 May the aircraft landed on the *Atlantic Conveyor,* already carrying the Sea Harrier aircraft of No. 809 Squadron. The ship sailed south, and on 18 May the Harrier and Sea Harrier warplanes lifted off from the ship to fly the last leg of their delivery to the aircraft carriers of the task force.

During the night of 3/4 May a Vulcan B.Mk 2 of No. 50 Squadron flew the second 'Black Buck' mission, but the bomber failed to hit the runway of BAM Malvinas. This failure was not a long-term augury, but in the short term 4 May was a good day for the Argentine air forces.

A post-attack reconnaissance photograph of BAM Malvinas (Stanley Airport) reveals the oblique row of bomb craters resulting from the first 'Black Buck' mission. The second 'Black Buck' mission failed to hit the runway

ENTER THE EXOCET

Given the importance that the Exocet missile possessed in the course of the Falklands war, it is useful to look slightly more closely at the actions in which this potentially decisive weapon was employed. The first of these actions, as described below, was the sinking of the destroyer *Sheffield* south-east of Lafonia on 4 May. Despite its equipment, which included an array of advanced sensors, the *Sheffield* received only the shortest of warnings of the missile's imminent arrival, and then only from a visual sighting. The missile's impact just above the waterline on the ship's starboard side started a major fire that eventually resulted in the abandonment and loss of the ship, whose crew lost 21 men dead. The event had a major effect on the tactical thinking of Admiral Woodward and his senior commanders, who decided that subsequent naval operations would have to be conducted in a manner that would reduce, as far as possible, the likelihood of other ships of the task force falling victim to this highly capable weapon.

A Sea King helicopter approaches the crippled 'Type 42' class destroyer HMS *Sheffield* after an Exocet anti-ship missile had hit her amidships on the starboard side on 4 May

The CANA had ordered 14 Super Etendard carrierborne interceptor and attack aircraft in 1979, together with a similar number of Exocet missiles. After personnel training in France, the first five of each were delivered to the BAN Comandante Espora at Bahia Blanca in November 1981, joining the 2 *Escuadrilla de Caza y Ataque* of the 3 *Escuadra Aeronaval.* As soon as it became clear that the United Kingdom was responding adversely to the Argentine invasion of the Falkland Islands, the training of the 2 *Escuadrilla,* potentially the most important asset of the Argentine naval air arm, was accelerated. France soon refused all further assistance, including the delivery of more aircraft and missiles, but

C-403 was the third Dagger received from Israel, and is seen here ready for take-off from San Julian with two 500-lb (227-kg) Mk 82 bombs and three drop tanks

it is possible that Israel provided aid in the solution of problems in the interfacing of the aircraft and their missiles. The Argentine pilots assiduously practised the skills of low-level navigation in radio and radar silence, and also the task of taking on fuel from the KC-130H Hercules tankers of the FAA. More direct tactical skills were honed in practice attacks on the Argentine navy's two British-supplied 'Type 42' class destroyers, of which the British task force eventually deployed five examples including the hapless *Sheffield.* After initial operational capability had been reached, 2 *Escuadrilla* moved to BAN Rio Grande on 19/20 April. This air base was the closest on the Argentine mainland to the Falkland Islands, but the task facing all the units based there is revealed by the fact that Port Stanley was nevertheless still some 440 miles (710 km) distant across the decidedly inhospitable waters of the South Atlantic.

On 2 May the 2 *Escuadrilla de Caza y Ataque's* commanding officer and his wing man, Commander Jorge Colombo and Lieutenant Carlos Machetanz, climbed into their aircraft in preparation for their first operational mission. The attack, undertaken using the tactical profile standard for all Super Etendard missions, involved a pair of aircraft each carrying one Exocet missile on the inner hardpoint under the starboard wing and one 242-Imp gal (1100-litre) drop tank under the port wing.

The Super Etendard mission planned for this day was schemed in concert with an attack by A-4Q Skyhawk carrierborne attack warplanes to divide the British defences and allow maximum effect from a planned pincer effort. As it was, the A-4Q aircraft were not launched as the major surface units of the Argentine navy retired to harbour in the aftermath of the sinking of the *General Belgrano* by a submarine-launched torpedo. No great success attended this first Super Etendard mission, the two aircraft returning to Rio Grande after the failure of an attempt to take on fuel from a KC-130H.

Two days later an SP-2H Neptune undertaking a reconnaissance of the waters around the Falkland Islands sighted and fixed the position of one

Operated from the carrier *Veinticinco de Mayo* and land bases, the A-4Q version of the Skyhawk attack bomber was the CANA's most potent warplane until the advent of the Super Etendard. The CANA received 16 such conversions from A-4B standard, this being the penultimate machine of the batch, in fact written off in June 1973

The CANA accepted its first five Super Etendards in November 1981

large and two small targets about 100 miles (160 km) to the south of Port Stanley. The 10 pilots of 2 *Escuadrilla de Caza y Ataque* had previously decided on a rotating schedule for Super Etendard missions, and 4 May saw the turn of Commander Augusto Bedacarratz together with Lieutenant Armando Mayora. Lifting off at 08.45 hours, the two pilots managed to top up their tanks from a KC-130H and then reduced height to just above the surface of the sea to prevent their detection by British radar. The bottom of the cloud cover was at a mere 500 ft (150 m) and the visibility was restricted to about 1,100 yards (1,000 m) as the two Argentine pilots flew toward the position of the British ships, en route receiving updated information from the SP-2H. This allowed the position of the largest ship to be loaded into the Exocet missile's guidance package. Wholly undetected by their target, the two Argentine aircraft climbed to 130 ft (40 m) in an unsuccessful effort to acquire the target on their own radars and then dropped down to 50 ft (15 m) once more. Even the very brief activation of the two Super Etendard warplanes' radars had been detected by British electronic support measures systems, and the *Sheffield's* report of air activity in her area was sufficient to cause the scrambling of two Sea Harrier fighters.

About 28 miles (45 km) farther along their course the two Argentine aircraft once more climbed briefly, and this time their radars found the targets, allowing updated position data to be fed to the Exocet missiles. Shortly after this the two Argentine pilots released their missiles, which both ignited their rocket motors and accelerated toward the British ships, whose identities had not been established. With their weapons committed to autonomous attacks, the pilots turned their Super Etendard warplanes west and headed for home.

Argentina had only five AM39 Exocets. An MM38 was also fired from Port Stanley, damaging HMS *Glamorgan*

From a range of between 23 and 35 miles (37 and 56 km), one of the Exocet missiles impacted the *Sheffield* as the ship steamed on radar picket duty some 25 miles (40 km) to the west of the task force's main body. The missile ripped a hole measuring about 10 ft (3.05 m) by 4 ft (1.2 m) in the side of the ship, and then there was, in the words of the captain, 'a short, sharp, unimpressive bang'. It is generally believed that the 364-lb (165-kg) high explosive warhead did not detonate, and that the explosion was in fact caused by the detonation of unburned rocket fuel. The *Sheffield* was soon burning strongly and was abandoned, sinking in the course of salvage efforts some six days later.

The second Exocet passed close to but did not home on the frigate *Yarmouth,* and soon fell into the sea after all its fuel had been burned.

The effective destruction and later sinking of the *Sheffield* were cause for great celebration in Argentina, but all was not well with the Super Etendard unit, or rather with the *Escuadrilla de Exploración,* on whose ancient SP-2H Neptune aircraft the 2 *Escuadrilla de Caza y Ataque* was almost wholly reliant for target detection and localisation. The last two SP-2H aircraft had to be taken out of service on 15 May, only two weeks after the start of overt hostilities, as now being ineffective and lacking in airworthiness. Unsuccessful efforts were then made to use an S-2 Tracker in the target location role, but thereafter the CANA had to employ educated guesswork in its efforts to find targets for its last three Exocet missiles. The fact was appreciated by the British, who developed the tactic of having their Sea Harrier fighters fly some 50 miles (80 km) from their carriers at very low level before climbing into the view of Falklands-based Argentine radars well away from their mother ships, which were the targets which the Argentines most urgently desired.

The Argentines then came to appreciate that the comparison of several aircraft tracks made it possible to 'guesstimate' the positions of the carriers with a reasonable level of accuracy. However, it was 23 May before the new concept could be tried operationally, and when the two Super Etendard warplanes climbed from their very low-level cruising flight regime to secure a radar image of the target, they found nothing and had to return to base.

The next mission was flown on Argentina's national day, 25 May, and after a delayed start resulting from lack of tanker availability, the two Super Etendard warplanes lifted off and started a roundabout flight designed to allow then to approach the ships of the task force from the

In the summer of 1979 the six S-2A Tracker carrierborne anti-submarine aircraft were retired from Argentine naval service, this move being made possible by the service's receipt in January 1978 of six improved S-2E aircraft surplus to the requirements of the US Navy. Seen in a low pass over a land base, 2-AS-5 was the fifth of the aircraft

north, an unexpected direction of attack. The Argentines believed that the main body of the task force was some 125 miles (200 km) to the north-east of Port Stanley, and flying east after they had taken on fuel, the two Super Etendard warplanes cruised at 628 mph (1,010 km/h) at a height of only 33 ft (10 m), and then turned south for the final leg estimated at 170 miles (275 km).

As the Argentine aircraft climbed briefly to locate their targets, the screens of their Agave radars indicated the presence of two large and one smaller ship. Position data were fed to the guidance packages of the two Exocet missiles, which were released at a range of about 35 miles (57 km). On the northern flank of the task force, the electronic support measures system of the frigate HMS *Ambuscade* 'heard' the transmissions of the Agave radars and issued an alert warning. The *Hermes,* which was the larger of the two British aircraft carriers, may have been the intended target, but quick action by the British decoy system prevented the missiles from securing any lock when they activated their own radars.

However, one of the missiles then locked onto the container ship *Atlantic Conveyor,* only 2 miles (3.2 km) from the *Hermes,* and struck the defenceless and unprotected ship in the side. The missile penetrated the ship's hull in the region where trucks and their fuel supplies were stored, resulting in an uncontrollable fire once the warhead had detonated. The ship burned out and went down five days later. British casualties were 12 men, and matériel losses included one Lynx, six Wessex and three Chinook helicopters, virtually all of the tents for the ground forces, spares and tools for Harrier and Sea Harrier warplanes, munitions including cluster bombs, and metal planking required for the creation of an advanced airstrip on East Falkland.

The Super Etendard pilot thought that the size of the echo on his radar screen indicated the presence of an aircraft carrier, which would have been a considerably more serious matter for the British. Even so, the sinking of the *Atlantic Conveyor* was a major blow, for the loss of helicopters embarked on her was critical and led to a major movement problem for the British troops on the inhospitable terrain in East Falkland.

Argentina now had only one Exocet missile left, and it was hoped that this could be successfully used in another long-range, circuitous mission similar to that which had led to the sinking of the *Atlantic Conveyor* in a mission that had lasted 3 hours 50 minutes and covered about 1,865 miles (3,000 km). This time the attack would be delivered from the south-east, but planning for the mission was complicated by the fact that the FAA demanded that four of its A-4 Skyhawk attack aircraft should also be part of the operation as 'payment' for the air force's allocation of KC-130H tankers to support the warplanes.

Although initially schemed for 29 May, the mission was in fact launched on the following day and comprised two Super Etendard warplanes (that without an Exocet missile operating as a radar reserve for the Exocet-armed machine) and

Seen here while refuelling from a KC-130H tanker on the outbound leg of the mission that resulted in the sinking of the *Atlantic Conveyor* on 25 May, 3-A-204 was flown by Teniente de Navio Julio Barraza as wing man to Capitán de Corbeta Roberto Curovilic flying the other Super Etendard

four Skyhawk machines. The aircraft took off from Rio Grande and some 50 minutes into the flight linked up with two KC-130H tankers, The eight aircraft flew in company for the next 217 miles (350 km) as the jet-powered warplanes took on fuel from the tankers at an altitude of some 19,685 ft (6,000 m). After the tankers had completed their part of the mission and broken away, the six warplanes descended to a height only marginally above the surface of the sea for the approach phase of the mission. Rain and low-lying cloud helped to obscure the aircraft from the possibility of visual detection, and a failed first radar 'pop up' was followed by a successful second effort, when the Super Etendard warplanes' radars acquired a large target at which the sole Exocet missile was launched.

At this point the two Super Etendard warplanes broke away from the formation, leaving the four Skyhawk machines to follow the Exocet. Two of the FAA's warplanes succumbed to the attentions of British surface-to-air missiles, and the other two later claimed that they had bombed the aircraft carrier *Invincible* from which, according to the surviving pilots, smoke was pouring from an apparent Exocet missile strike. The ship which the two Skyhawk attack aircraft had attacked was in fact the frigate HMS *Avenger,* which was turning away from the threat and making smoke. Believing that their attack of 25 May had damaged if not sunk the *Hermes,* the men of 2 *Escuadrilla de Caza y Ataque* believed that they had crippled the second British aircraft carrier, which might yet sink.

The reality of the situation was somewhat different. Having received timely warning of the impending attacks, the ships of the task force had been ready to use the full range of their countermeasures. The *Avenger* was in any event some 29 miles (46 km) from the *Invincible* and thus well out of Exocet range, and the destroyer *Exeter* claimed to have downed an Exocet at a range of 14,900 yards (12,800 m): it is altogether more likely that the missile was diverted by the British countermeasures, expended its fuel and fell into the sea.

Lacking further Exocet missiles, 2 *Escuadrilla de Caza y Ataque* was now pulled out of action. This is a strange decision for the CANA to have made, for the aircraft could have been used to possibly telling effect as fighter-bombers or even as escorts for other bomb-carrying aircraft in attacks on the beach-head that the British had established on 21 May. The reason for this is problematical, but the most likely reason is that the Argentine navy wished to see no diminution of its most prized air assets at a time when hopes of eventual victory were starting to fade and the losses of the FAA to British fighters and surface-to-air missiles were revealing the improbability of success in the air over the Falkland Islands.

It is worth noting that the whole episode leading to the loss of the *Sheffield* revealed a major vulnerability of the task force's ships to attacks by advanced anti-ship missiles launched from low-flying warplanes that could not be detected, and therefore tackled and destroyed, for lack of any airborne early warning radar system. This had disappeared a few years earlier, when the decision to phase out the Royal Navy's last large aircraft carriers had led to the retirement of the last Fairey Gannet AEW (Airborne Early Warning) aircraft. A hasty effort was launched to create a radar picket version of the Sea King helicopter, but this Sea King AEW.Mk 2 did not become available until after the end of the Falklands war, in which the ships of the task force were therefore at a major disadvantage.

THE BATTLE FOR EAST FALKLAND

Another loss on 4 May, the day the Sheffield was hit, occurred when Lieutenant N. Taylor of No. 800 Squadron was killed when his Sea Harrier was downed by ground-based anti-aircraft fire during a raid on BAM Condor at Goose Green. The following morning two pilots of No. 801 Squadron were posted as missing, it being believed that their Sea Harrier warplanes had collided at low-level as the two pilots searched for a contact near the abandoned hulk of the *Sheffield.* It was not that the day brought nothing but bad news to the British, however, for on 4 May the Argentine navy's potentially most threatening surface unit, the aircraft carrier ARA *Veinticinco de Mayo* (25 May) returned to port with apparent engine problems, and remained there for the rest of the war. At the time of the Falklands war, the ship's air wing of 18 fixed- and four rotary-wing aircraft comprised a varying blend of A-4Q Skyhawk attack and S-2E Tracker anti-submarine aircraft as well as S-61D Sea King medium and SA.316B Alouette III light multi-role helicopters. The Argentine navy's decision to withdraw the ship to harbour may have saved her from destruction by British warships and/or aircraft, but before that time her air strength could have posed a severe danger to the ships of the British task force. The ship's A-4 Skyhawk attack aircraft transferred to BAN Rio Grande for land-based use.

Over the next few days poor weather severely hampered flying operations, but even so the Sea Harrier warplanes of the British aircraft carriers maintained their combat air patrols in case the Argentines tried to slip an

Of these four A-4Q warplanes on board the carrier ARA *Veinticinco de Mayo* on 1 May, one is armed with obsolete AIM-9B Sidewinder air-to-air missiles for emergency air defence use, while the other three are each being armed with six 500-lb (227-kg) Mk 82 'Snakeye' retarded bombs

Soon after this photograph was taken on 9 May, this A-4C and its pilot, Teniente Jorge Farias of *Grupo 4,* were lost in unknown circumstances during a sortie against the British task force off East Falkland. Another A-4C, C-313 flown by Teniente Jorge Casco, was lost on the same mission when it hit cliffs on South Jason Island

attack through the weather in an effort to catch the British off their guard.

During this period the cruise liner *Canberra* departed Ascension Island on 8 May, and from a time three days later the task force enjoyed the benefits of improved long-range cover from the advent of No. 206 Squadron's Nimrod MR.Mk 2P aircraft, – the 'P' suffix indicating the inflight-refuelling probe recently fitted to the type for a significant enhancement of operational radius when flying from Wideawake Airfield.

Several A-4C attack warplanes of *Grupo 4 de Caza* took off from San Julian on 9 May in an attempt to find and bomb British warships, but the unit suffered its first two losses of the war when two Skyhawk aircraft succumbed to the weather on the outward legs of their sorties. On the same day CAB 601 lost a Puma helicopter to a Sea Dart medium/long-range surface-to-air missile fired by the destroyer HMS *Coventry* over Choiseul Sound, and naval gunfire also damaged a UH-1H helicopter at Moody Brook. Sea Harrier warplanes of No. 800 Squadron attacked the *Narwhal,* an intelligence-gathering trawler used by the Argentine navy, which was then boarded by men of the Special Boat Service delivered by Sea King helicopters.

On 12 May the pilots of *Grupo 5* thought that they had sunk the 'Type 22' class destroyer HMS *Brilliant,* and this A-4B was marked with a ship silhouette below the serial under the cockpit. In fact the *Brilliant* had escaped without damage, although in the same attack the 'Type 42' class destroyer HMS *Glasgow* was modestly damaged by a bomb that passed right through the ship without exploding

Meanwhile the naval bombardment of the Argentine positions around Port Stanley continued, but during 12 May the destroyer HMS *Glasgow* and the frigate *Brilliant* were attacked by A-4B warplanes of *Grupo 5 de Caza,* and a 500-lb (227-kg) bomb that failed to explode nonetheless effectively put the *Glasgow* out of action. The fusing of its bombs was a major problem for the FAA throughout the war, for the bombs were generally fused for release at altitudes higher than those at which they were in fact dropped, and the result was that the bombs often lacked the time to arm themselves before hitting their targets, which thus escaped with kinetic rather than blast/fragmentation damage. The attackers paid a high price for the damage they inflicted on the *Glasgow,* however, for they lost two of their number to Seawolf short-range surface-to-air missiles fired by the *Brilliant,* a third Skyhawk hit the sea, and a fourth was shot down by Argentine 35-mm anti-aircraft guns. The sole British loss of the day was a Sea King helicopter of No. 826 Squadron, which came down in the sea as a result of engine failure.

The potential for further ground force strength was meanwhile leaving the United Kingdom in the form of the liner *Queen Elizabeth 2,* which departed from Southampton with the 5th Infantry Brigade and steamed straight for South Georgia, where it was planned that the troops would be transferred to smaller and less vulnerable ships for onward delivery to the Falkland Islands.

On 13 May 'Black Buck 3' was called off as headwinds would have made the mission extremely difficult in terms of fatigue for the Vulcan bomber's crew and the very large quantities of fuel that would have been needed, plus the additional flight hours that would have accrued to the already overextended Victor tankers.

The night of 14 May was notable for the delivery onto Pebble Island by Sea King helicopters of No. 846 Squadron of an SAS party. Before dawn on 15 May, the men of this party launched an attack on EA Calderon to destroy or cripple six Pucará warplanes as well as four T-34C-1 machines of 4 *Escuadrilla de Ataque* and one Skyvan transport, before pulling out without any losses.

Operating from Ascension Island, a Nimrod MR.Mk 2P set a record for an operational sortie, covering some 8,300 miles (13,355 km) in a flying time of 19 hours 5 minutes in the course of a mission to check Argentine naval positions.

As the time for invasion approached, Sea Harrier warplanes harried Argentine ships off the coast of the Falkland Islands, scoring successes on 16 May when they damaged the *Rio Carcarona* and *Bahia Buen Suceso.* On the following day, though, the British lost two helicopters when a Sea King HAS.Mk 5 of No. 826 Squadron came down in the water after its radar altimeter failed in the course of a sonar search, and a Sea King HC.Mk 4 of No. 846 Squadron was deliberately set on fire and destroyed by its crew at Agua Fresca near Punta Arenas, Chile, after a one-way sortie associated with the insertion of an SAS party. The sortie was possibly to sabotage Argentine aircraft or more probably to report on Argentine aircraft movements, most particularly the take-off of Super Etendard attack warplanes from BAN Rio Grande. The dismal weather conditions also led to the loss of another helicopter and the deaths of all 21 men on board it: this was a Sea King HC.Mk 4 of No. 846

Pictured on 21 May, the date on which the British landing on East Falkland was committed, this Sea King HC.Mk 4 is carrying an underslung load of equipment and supplies for the troops in the beach-head on the eastern edge of San Carlos Water. In the background are the P&O cruise liner *Canberra,* which was used as a troop transport in the campaign, and just behind the ship another Sea King helicopter

Squadron that hit a bird as it was moving troopers of the SAS from the *Hermes* to the *Intrepid.*

The British amphibious landing force now linked with the battle force off to the north-west of the Falkland Islands, and the landing was now fixed for 21 May in San Carlos Water on the western side of East Falkland's north section. In the course of the operations to discommode the Argentine defence before the landing was launched, the Harrier GR.Mk 3 warplanes of No. 1 Squadron undertook their first sorties against installations at Goose Green, destroying a fuel dump. On 20 May the whole British task force steamed into the region bounded by the Total

Harrier GR.Mk 3 close support warplanes had initially to operate from the decks of the aircraft carriers to aid the forces landed on East Falkland, but were redeployed to an extemporised airstrip ashore as soon as possible, allowing a shorter reaction time in action and freeing the carriers' decks for Sea Harrier operations

Exclusion Zone, and after the troops had been transferred to their assault transports the first landings of Operation 'Sutton' were undertaken. Just before dawn on 21 May the first landing in San Carlos Water was made by 2 Para. It was highly probable that the first reports of the British landings would spur the Argentines into a major effort, by air and possibly by sea if not by land, and as a result the warships of the task force had moved into San Carlos Water to provide both gunfire support for the landed troops and anti-aircraft support (with missiles and guns) against any intervention by Argentine aircraft. The ships moved into San Carlos Water under cover of heavy mist, but even so had been detected and reported by a Canberra bomber of the FAA.

Just before the pace of events started to accelerate in San Carlos Water with troops landing and ships arriving in larger numbers, a Nimrod MR.Mk 2P of No. 206 Squadron took off from Ascension Island in the early hours of the day on a sortie that was to set another record. The aeroplane flew 8,453 miles (13,603 km) to provide surveillance of Argentine naval operations, the crew's specific task being the reporting of any movements that might offer a threat to the forces in San Carlos Water. At much the same time SAS and SBS elements launched diversionary attacks on the Argentines' Goose Green and Darwin garrisons to the south-east of San Carlos Water. Despite the fact that the landings were progressing without problem and the beach-head was being extended inland against no opposition, the commanders afloat appreciated that there was considerable urgency required in the establishment of a high-quality defence, on shore as well as on the water, before the inevitable Argentine air riposte arrived.

With the fighters of the Sea Harrier force providing top cover and combat air patrols, the Harrier warplanes attacked an Argentine helicopter concentration on Mount Kent, just to the west of Port Stanley, from where reinforcements could have been flown to the beach-head to oppose the British landing: at about 08.00 hours a Puma and a CH-47C were destroyed by gunfire. However, it was not long after this before the British also began to suffer losses: a Harrier GR.Mk 3 on an armed reconnaissance mission over Port Howard, on the eastern shore of West Falkland across Falkland Sound from San Carlos Water, was hit by a Blowpipe shoulder-launched surface-to-air missile and its pilot, Flight Lieutenant J. Glover, ejected; and near the beach-head, two Aérospatiale Gazelle helicopters of the 3rd Commando Brigade Air Squadron were downed in quick succession during the course of a mission supporting a Sea King sortie. Both Gazelle pilots lost their lives, and it was immediately apparent that the Gazelle would be of only limited use over the battlefield as the type was clearly vulnerable to small arms fire.

A Pucará light attack warplane sighted the invasion force at about 10.00 hours on 21 May, just after another Pucará had been destroyed by a Stinger shoulder-launched surface-to-air missile launched by a member of an SAS party. A single

The 68-mm (2.68-in) SNEB air-to-surface unguided rocket was tested on Gazelle AH.Mk 1 helicopters of No. 3 Commando Brigade Air Squadron off Ascension Island, but was not used operationally over the Falkland Islands largely because the helicopter pilots felt the weapon lacked the accuracy required to avoid casualties among friendly ground troops

It was planned that the Gazelle AH.Mk 1 light helicopter would provide a scouting and light attack capability in support of the troops landed on East Falkland, as well as the casualty evacuation capability here revealed, but the type was hampered by its lightweight structure and single-engined powerplant, which made the helicopter vulnerable to ground fire

Aermacchi MB-339A then attacked the frigate HMS *Argonaut,* causing only light damage. These poorly executed first attacks on the invasion force had been undertaken on an almost ad hoc basis by light warplanes based in the Falkland Islands, but news of the landings had been relayed to the Argentine command on the mainland, where a more ambitious and determined air effort was quickly launched. The first attack from mainland bases reached San Carlos Water at 10.25 hours, when A-4B Skyhawk attack warplanes of the *Grupo 5 de Caza* and Dagger fighters of the *Grupo 6 de Caza* arrived on the scene. The incoming aircraft were spotted neither visually nor by radar, and were thus able to make effectively unhampered attacks on the *Antrim* and *Argonaut,* which were disabled. The sole Argentine loss of the raid was a single Dagger which splashed into the water after being hit by a Seawolf surface-to-air missile fired by the *Brilliant.*

Two A-4B Skyhawk warplanes of *Grupo 5* link up for the final stage of their approach to targets on or round the Falkland Islands after topping up their tanks from a KC-130H tanker

The British air position over the landing was hampered by the fact that the two British aircraft carriers had been pulled back well to the east, out of range of direct Argentine air attack. This may well have made the ships safer, but it also meant that in the absence of any inflight-refuelling capability and the need to operate from two ships well distant from San Carlos Water, each Sea Harrier fighter could operate for only a short time over San Carlos Water and the beach-head. Without an airborne early warning aircraft, and therefore any 'look-down' radar cover, the British ships supporting the landing had to depend for raid warnings on the surveillance radar of ships posted as pickets for this purpose. These ships were therefore notably exposed to air attack, and at about 12.00 hours the frigate HMS *Ardent* came under attack by Pucará warplanes of the *Grupo 3 de Ataque,* one of which fell over Lafonia (the southern half of the land mass whose northern half is East Falkland) to the devastating hits of the 30-mm cannon fire of a Sea Harrier of No. 801 Squadron. The next attack on the ships came about one hour later, and was launched by A-4 attack warplanes of the mainland-based *Grupos 4* and *5 de Caza.* However, by this time the British aircraft carriers had been able to increase the numbers of Sea Harrier fighters available in the combat air patrol task, and although one A-4 inflicted a measure of damage on the *Ardent,* two others were shot down by AIM-9L Sidewinder missiles launched by Sea Harrier fighters of No. 800 Squadron.

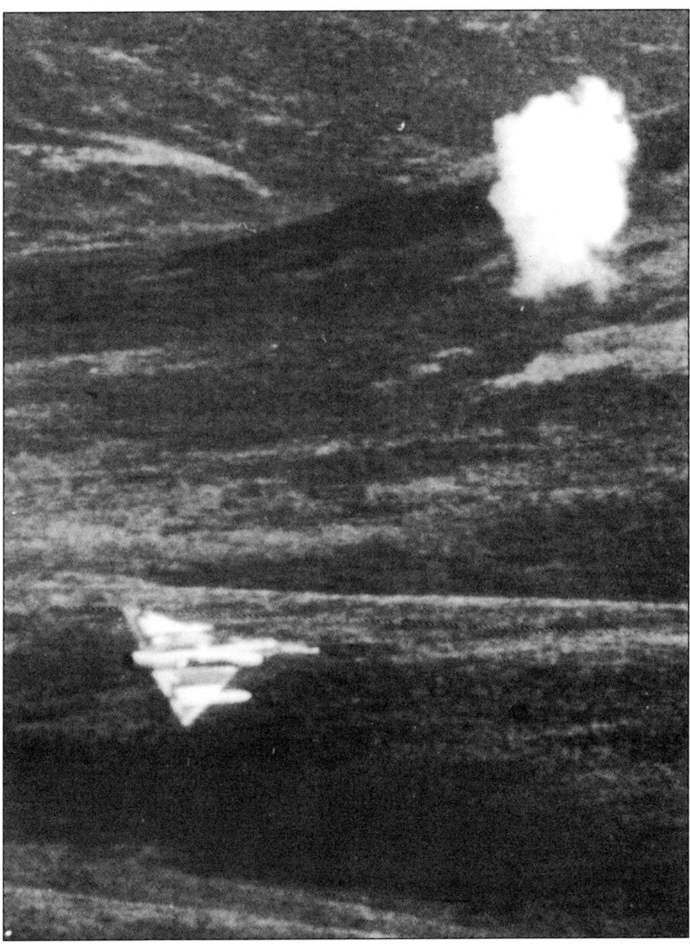

Silhouetted against the land behind it, a Dagger streaks through naval AA gunfire over San Carlos Water on 21 May

The third mainland-launched raid of the day arrived at 14.35 hours as

Framed through the windscreen of a companion aeroplane, these are three A-4B warplanes of *Grupo 5*

Dagger warplanes of the *Grupo 6 de Caza* streamed into the attack at low level, their approach masked from detection by the British ships' radar until the last minute by the height of the land round San Carlos Water. Even so, one Dagger was destroyed on its run-in to the target by the attentions of a Sea Harrier of No. 800 Squadron. Another Dagger inflicted more damage on the already hit *Ardent* and destroyed the ship's Lynx helicopter. Fifteen minutes later a second wave of Argentine aircraft was caught by the Sea Harrier fighters of No. 801 Squadron, which downed all three of the aircraft with their Sidewinder missiles.

Despite the courage and determination with which they had pressed home their attacks, the first series of attacks by mainland-based aircraft of the FAA in fact achieved little in the way of concrete results, largely as a result of the poor performance of the bombs being dropped. These were generally older weapons of indifferent performance, or newer weapons that were still inadequately fused.

At this stage the CANA started to make its presence felt. At 15.10 hours A-4Q attack warplanes of the 3 *Escuadrilla de Caza y Ataque* launched their first attack, in this instance with retarded rather than free-fall bombs. The first objective of the attack was again the *Ardent,* and on this occasion the luckless frigate received severe damage, sinking on the next day. The balance was slightly redressed, so far as the British were concerned, by the fact that Sea Harrier fighters of No. 801 Squadron destroyed two of the Skyhawk warplanes and severely damaged a third whose pilot, before finally ejecting after attempting a landing, had tried to make BAM Malvinas at Port Stanley rather than attempt the long overwater flight back to the mainland.

By the end of 21 May the Argentine air forces had between them lost 12 warplanes and two helicopters, with four pilots killed, while the British losses for the same period had amounted to one Harrier and three helicopters, with two pilots killed. In overall terms, though, the Argentine air forces had succeeded in destroying one frigate, disabling a destroyer and inflicting damage on three other frigates.

There was a lull in the air fighting on 22 May as a result of the weather over the mainland, and this worked to the advantage of the British, who

On 21 May the Dagger warplanes of *Grupo 6* flew five attacks on the British ships in San Carlos Water for the launch of the land invasion, this being an abortive attack on the assault transport HMS *Fearless.* Throughout the day the FAA had sought to fly 63 sorties against the invasion force but achieved only 53 of these, in the process losing seven aircraft for an unsustainable loss rate of 13%. *Grupo 6* had flown 23 escort and attack sorties during the day, in the process losing five aircraft for the appalling loss rate of 22%. The Dagger warplanes had damaged the destroyer HMS *Antrim,* the frigate HMS *Ardent* and other ships to a lesser degree

The bow of the 'Type 21' class frigate HMS *Antelope* rises above the water as the burning ship sinks on 24 May in San Carlos Water. On the previous day the ship had been hit by two 1,000-lb (454-kg) bombs from two of four A-4B Skyhawk warplanes flown by pilots of *Grupo 5*. The first and second bombs hit the ship's after and forward sections respectively, but had been dropped from so low an altitude that neither weapon had armed itself. The ship was temporarily abandoned, but as a bomb disposal team worked on the bomb in the after section it exploded and set the ship on fire. A subsequent explosion tore the ship into two parts which sank on the following day

A Dagger streaks low over the water above the LSL RFA *Sir Bedivere* in San Carlos Water during the 24 May attack on the British shipping supporting the landings that had been made on 21 May. The aeroplane is one of the day's first wave of four attackers, which escaped without too much interference, and is probably C-431 flown by Capitán Carlos Maffeis

were thus able to land more men, equipment and supplies even as Harrier warplanes attacked BAM Condor outside Goose Green.

A higher pace of air operations resumed on 23 May, starting at 10.30 hours when a Sea Harrier combat air patrol caught sight of Argentine helicopters attempting to move supplies over West Falkland. The pilots of No. 801 Squadron made several attacks on the helicopters, shooting down one Agusta A 109A and two Puma machines. It was only in the afternoon that the first attacks on the British ships in Falkland Sound and San Carlos Water arrived, when just before 14.00 hours A-4 Skyhawk warplanes of the *Grupo 5 de Caza* struck the frigate HMS *Antelope:* the ship sustained some damage in the attack, but was mortally wounded after the end of the attack when an unexploded bomb inside the hull detonated as an attempt was being made to defuse it. During the raid, a ship-launched surface-to-air missile destroyed an A-4B, and in the course of a later attack a Sea Harrier of No. 800 Squadron destroyed one Dagger. However, in the early evening of the same day the British suffered the loss of one Sea Harrier of No. 800 Squadron when it hit the sea and exploded shortly after lifting off for a toss-bombing mission.

The British ships in Falkland Sound and San Carlos Water were now subjected to a number of attacks. On 24 May, for example, the Argentines had lost three Dagger and one A-4C Skyhawk aircraft, the Dagger machines all to the attentions of No. 800 Squadron's Sea Harrier fighters and the Skyhawk to naval gunfire.

C-430 and C-419, whose tail is just visible in the background, were the two Dagger warplanes shot down by the Sea Harrier of No. 801 Squadron's Lieutenant Commander Auld on 24 May

During 25 May the British suffered one of their most grievous warship losses. The destroyer HMS *Coventry* was attacked by aircraft of the *Grupos 4* and *5 de Caza* while serving as a radar picket to the west of the Falkland Islands. The ship destroyed two of her attackers (single examples of the A-4B and A-4C) with Sea Dart surface-to-air missiles, but was herself struck and sank shortly after this. British naval gunfire destroyed a third Skyhawk in San Carlos Water.

By 27 May the British forces had secured their beach-head, and the time was now ripe for the initial break-out toward Goose Green by 2 Para. Shortly before the breakout of 2 Para from the San Carlos beach-head, the Argentine garrison at Goose Green had been strengthened by the airlift of reinforcements of the Argentine army's 12th Regiment from Mount Kent. Thus the fighting for Goose Green on 27 May was harder than it would otherwise have been, and the men on the ground were able to enjoy only limited assistance from the close support capability of the Harrier.

The 'Type 42' class destroyer HMS *Coventry* billows smoke after being hit by bombs from an A-4B on 25 May

The five 'Type 42' class guided missile destroyers allocated to the British task force were intended to provide a multi-role capability including medium-range defence of the two aircraft carriers against aircraft attack, but lost two of their number, HMS *Coventry* and HMS *Sheffield,* to Argentine air attack, while HMS *Glasgow* was also damaged. This is the *Coventry,* which lost 19 men killed in the attack

On one such sortie, Squadron Leader R. Iveson was hit over Goose Green and ejected. Iveson was able to hide from the Argentines for three days before being located and extracted by a Gazelle of the 3rd Commando Brigade Air Squadron. Over the same period further Argentine air attacks on the British ships were severely handled, the attackers losing one A-4B to gunfire, two Pucará machines to small arms fire, and one MB-339A to a Blowpipe surface-to-air missile while attempting to cripple ships and landed troops. A date notable in the history of the Falklands war was 28 May, for on this day Pucará aircraft made the only (and unsuccessful) use of napalm in the campaign. The same day also witnessed the shooting down by a Pucará of a Westland Scout AH.Mk 1 helicopter of the 3rd Commando Brigade Air Squadron in the course of a casualty evacuation mission.

The British still felt that the Argentine air assets deployed, or indeed deployable, to BAM Malvinas at Port Stanley could pose a longer-term threat to the British advance across East Falkland toward the island's main town, and as a result two Vulcan bombers adapted for the carriage and firing of the AGM-45 Shrike anti-radar missile were deployed to Ascension Island with a view to destruction of the radar on which the Argentines were reliant for effective use of the airfield. The next effort to render BAM Malvinas inoperable was a conventional bombing mission, but this 'Black Buck 4' sortie had to be called off some five hours after the Vulcan had taken off because of the failure of a hose-and-drogue refuelling unit on one of the essential Victor support aircraft.

During an attack on 25 May by A-4B warplanes of *Grupo 5* on the 'Type 22' class destroyer HMS *Broadsword,* a bomb passed through the flight platform of the destroyer, in the process roughly shearing off the nose of a Lynx HAS.Mk 2

On East Falkland, No. 45 Commando and 3 Para broke out of the San Carlos beach-head and undertook a march of epic endurance under very adverse weather conditions toward Port Stanley via Douglas and Teal Inlet. This was the northern element of the two-axis British advance on Port Stanley, the southern element being headed by 2 Para from Goose Green, and air support was provided by the Harrier warplanes of No. 1 Squadron. This air support was needed most strongly in the area around Mount Kent, but was forcibly curtailed by appalling weather. Lack of adequate helicopter strength meant that the advance had to be undertaken in the old-fashioned way, by foot, the available helicopter strength being used to bring up limited reinforcements and supplies, and to evacuate casualties. By this time the Argentine air resistance over the islands had dwindled to virtually nothing, and though the Sea Harrier fighters still provided cover for British ships and the advancing troops with their limited air support, there was little 'trade' for the naval pilots. Even so, one Sea Harrier was lost in an accident on 29 May, and three days later a Roland surface-to-air missile brought down another Sea Harrier, whose pilot ejected safely but then spent many hours in the sea before being lifted to safety by a Sea King helicopter of No. 820 Squadron. One British success of the period was the destruction of a C-130E of the *Grupo 1 de Transporte Aereo,* which a Sea Harrier of No. 801 Squadron shot down on 1 June after the lumbering

With a Wessex helicopter hovering in the background, this is a Gazelle AH.Mk 1 of No. 656 Squadron over East Falkland with multi-tube launchers for 68-mm (2.68-in) SNEB air-to-surface unguided rockets

Protection of landed troops against Argentine air attack was entrusted to Blowpipe short-range surface-to-air missiles, which were shoulder-launched weapons, and to the 12 Rapier four-arm missile launchers of T Battery of the 3rd Commando Brigade's 12th Air Defence Regiment

transport had departed from BAM Malvinas on a mission to locate and identify British ships. There were still some air attacks on British ships, as suggested by the Hercules' mission, but the Argentines suffered the loss of one Dagger to a Rapier short-range surface-to-air missile from a land-based launcher in the course of 29 May, and on the following day two A-4C warplanes of the *Grupo 4 de Caza* succumbed to Sea Dart surface-to-air missiles from the destroyer HMS *Exeter.* The Skyhawk machines fell in the course of the last Exocet attack, which was directed at the carrier *Invincible,* but it seems likely that the weapon's rocket motor burned out after the missile had been decoyed away from its target.

A type that was technically obsolescent in the Falklands war was the Scout AH.Mk 1, the British army's counterpart to the Royal Navy's Wasp HAS.Mk 1 with different equipment and twin-skid rather than quadricycle landing gear. The 3rd Commando Brigade's Air Squadron had 11 Gazelle and six Scout helicopters, while the 5th Infantry Brigade's No. 656 Squadron had six Gazelle and three Scout helicopters. Casualties are being loaded into the Scout depicted here

Despite its receipt of significant arms shipments from Israel and arrival of Ecuadorian, Peruvian and Uruguayan aircraft, Argentina was wholly unable to procure further examples of the Exocet, which was perhaps the only weapon that could have won the war for Argentina by destroying or crippling the two aircraft carriers on which the British forces in and around the Falkland Islands were wholly dependent.

Seen at Wideawake Airfield on Ascension Island is a Vulcan B.Mk 2 carrying a simply camouflaged AGM-45 Shrike anti-radar missile. Two of the last three 'Black Buck' missions flown by the Vulcan force were directed at Argentine radar installations on East Falkland

Lack of any heavy-lift helicopter capability but the resources of a single Chinook twin-rotor machine meant that rapid tactical movement had to be expedited by any and all means available. This Scout AH.Mk 1 carries, in addition to its two-man crew, a casualty litter on the starboard side of the main landing gear and four soldiers in the rear of the cabin, one of them half out of the port door

OVERALL BRITISH AIR SUPERIORITY

Argentine attacks on British ships now ended for the period until 8 June, largely as a result of the bad weather that was also affecting the operations of the Harrier aircraft seeking to support the British land advance. Whenever possible, the Harrier aircraft undertook armed reconnaissance and close support sorties, the aircraft often taking hits from small arms fire as they had to operate at very low level for weather as well as tactical reasons. One Harrier was lost on 30 May after a fuel line had been hit, its pilot ejecting short of the *Hermes.*

The British situation began to improve from 2 June, with the opening of a forward operating base at Port San Carlos allowing the deployment of some aircraft to this land base, removing the need for over-water flights and also increasing the time that the Harrier warplanes could spend over their targets.

The first anti-radar mission by a Vulcan bomber equipped with Shrike missiles was 'Black Buck 5' on 31 May, but the attack caused only minimal damage. 'Black Buck 6', flown on 3 June, enjoyed somewhat greater success as it caused damage to a Skyguard fire-control radar, but

A Sea King HAS.Mk 2, one of many anti-submarine helicopters pressed into service as transport machines, flies over a battery of 105-mm (4.13-in) L118A1 Light Guns on its way to deliver a slung load of supplies

after its inflight-refuelling probe broke the Vulcan had no option but to divert to Rio de Janeiro, the capital of Brazil, where it was interned for some nine days before being released.

By the start of June, the 5th Infantry Brigade was landing at San Carlos and, under the supervision of Major General Jeremy Moore, the land force commander, the British started on the movement of parts of 2 Para from the Goose Green area to Fitzroy and Bluff Cove, small settlements just to the south-west of Port Stanley. With only one Chinook helicopter available, it was decided that further strength for the southern arm of the advance on Port Stanley, in the form of the Scots and Welsh Guards, would be moved up by ship. Even so, two Chinook sorties on 2 June moved forward 156 men of 2 Para. Bad weather was a continual impediment to the effective use of air power, but even so several types of helicopters operated over East Falkland to bring up equipment and supplies and fly out casualties as the Royal Marines and the men of the Parachute Regiment drove forward toward Port Stanley. The weather was not the only problem for the helicopters, moreover, as evidenced by the fact that on 6 June a Gazelle machine of No. 656 Squadron was lost (possibly to British naval gunfire) while trying to deliver supplies to the men around Mount Pleasant.

The extended duration and continued pace of operations in and around the Falkland Islands meant that a continuous flow of supplies was needed, and to bolster the efforts of a small fleet of ships Hercules transport aircraft were employed to paradrop vital supplies to the task force's ships at the far end of very long-endurance and multiple air-refuelled flights from and back to Ascension Island. Moreover, extra Harrier warplanes for No. 1 Squadron completed long deployment flights from Wideawake Airfield direct to the *Hermes,* again with the aid of the extraordinarily hard-working tankers of the RAF.

The Argentine air forces were still trying to exert an influence on the course of events, and within this effort the FAA undertook several night

Photographed during their return to Rio Grande from the Learjet 35A that provided pathfinder support for the mission, are two of the five Dagger warplanes that attacked the 'Rothesay' class frigate HMS *Plymouth* on 8 June. Between 1 May and 13 June, the Dagger warplanes of *Grupo 6* flew 133 out of a planned total of 160 sorties, 88 of them leading to combat in which the Dagger force lost 11 of its number resulting in the deaths of five pilots and the safe ejections of the other six

A Sea King helicopter inches its way forward toward the blazing stern of RFA *Sir Galahad* burning off Fitzroy on 8 June. The helicopter's rescue man is on the end of the wire under the helicopter as the pilot tries to use the rotor downwash to blow inflatable life rafts away from the ship

RFA *Sir Galahad,* an LSL manned by the Royal Fleet Auxiliary and caught while trying to unload men of the 2nd Battalion The Welsh Guards at Fitzroy, burns after being hit by three bombs from the A-4B Skyhawk of *Grupo 5's* Primer Teniente Cachón. The bombs hit the ship's after part and all exploded, causing a fire and the detonation of ammunition in board. The ship burned for a week after being hit on 8 June, and was later towed away and sunk by the British on 26 June as a war grave

bombing missions against Port San Carlos using its obsolescent Canberra B.Mk 62 bombers. Reconnaissance data for the planning of such missions was difficult to obtain, though, and on 7 June a Sea Dart surface-to-air missile from the destroyer *Exeter* claimed another Argentine victim in the form of a Learjet business transport adapted for the reconnaissance role and brought down over Pebble Island.

The fact that the Argentine air forces had not shot their bolt was forcibly brought home to the British on 8 June. For lack of adequate helicopter strength, the British had decided to take the risk of moving men of the two Guards regiments to Fitzroy by sea. Nothing in the way of air cover could be provided, the passage to Fitzroy lacked any natural cover, and there were Argentine positions with a clear line of sight to the selected anchorage at Port Pleasant. The assault ships *Fearless* and *Intrepid,* together with the LSLs *Sir Galahad* and *Sir Tristram,* were used for the deliveries of men onto this southern axis of the advance on Port Stanley.

The Argentine forces in the area inevitably reported the progress of events, and a major effort was planned against the ships and their embarked troops. By 8 June better weather had arrived, and thus greatly aided the Argentine command in its planning of several waves of attacks.

In the first of these waves, *Grupo 5 de Caza* was to launch eight of its A-4B attack warplanes under the cover of six Dagger fighters provided by

Damaged and abandoned on 8 June after an air attack, the LSL RFA *Sir Tristram* was later reboarded and salvaged. The attack was delivered off Fitzroy by a pair of A-4B Skyhawk attack warplanes flown by Teniente Galvez and Alferez Gomez of *Grupo 5.* The aircraft each carried three 500-lb (227-kg) bombs. The bombs dropped by Gomez fell short while those released by Galvez struck home, but of these three weapons only one detonated

the *Grupo 6 de Caza,* with four Mirage IIIEA fighters of *Grupo 8 de Caza* making a slightly earlier raid on the San Carlos area to draw off the standard combat air patrol of Sea Harrier fighters. Inflight-refuelling difficulties trimmed the A-4B force from eight to five aircraft, but these reached the target area at 13.50 hours, when they attacked the two LSLs with bombs, several of which hit the *Sir Galahad.* The bomb explosions were followed by a raging fire, resulting in the deaths of 43 men of the Welsh Guards as well as seven sailors, and severe injuries to many more. The other LSL, the *Sir Tristram,* was also badly damaged in the same attack.

The British immediately began a major rescue effort in which the Sea King helicopters of No. 825 Squadron, which had been involved in the off-loading of stores from the ships, played a decisive role. This squadron had been commissioned only on 7 May at Royal Naval Air Station (RNAS) Culdrose with Sea King HAS.Mk 2 anti-submarine helicopters rapidly adapted to transport layout, and had reached the Falkland Islands only recently to ease the task of the completely overextended No. 846 Squadron.

While traversing Falkland Sound, moreover, the Dagger fighters escorting the A-4B machines found the frigate *Plymouth* in an exposed location and attacked the ship, inflicting sufficient damage to disable her. The Mirage IIIEA diversion also succeeded in drawing off the Sea Harrier fighters, and then used their superior speed to escape the British warplanes as they tried to close to missile-launch range. All the Argentine warplanes returned safely to their bases at the end of an operation that must be reckoned a major Argentine success.

The day's second attack was schemed for 16.45 hours, and involved

Attended by the 'Type 21' frigate HMS *Avenger* and silhouetted in front of a hovering Sea King helicopter, the 'Rothesay' class frigate HMS *Plymouth* is severely damaged on 8 June near Fitzroy by Dagger warplanes of *Grupo 6* operating in the fighter-bomber role with a Learjet 35A as their pathfinder. Five of the six Dagger warplanes that took off from Rio Grande, each carrying two 500-lb (227-kg) Mk 82 bombs, attacked the *Plymouth*, hitting the ship with five out of eight bombs. None of these exploded, but a 30-mm cannon shell hit the stern of the ship and caused a depth charge to explode causing a fire

four A-4B warplanes of the *Grupo 5 de Caza* against British ships alongside four A-4C warplanes of the *Grupo 4 de Caza* carrying anti-personnel bombs, with a force of Mirage IIIEA fighters as cover. The first raid had alerted the British to the possibility of follow-on Argentine efforts, however, and the defences were now on a high state of alert. Thus while one A-4B succeeded in destroying a landing craft from the *Fearless* between Fitzroy and Goose Green, the Sea Harrier fighters of No. 800 Squadron rapidly downed three Argentine aircraft over Choiseul Sound, the channel separating East Falkland proper from Lafonia, its southern half. The aircraft of the *Grupo 4 de Caza* escaped but inflicted no damage, but the Mirage IIIEA fighters, their pilots now fully aware of the tactical advantage enjoyed by the Sea Harrier/Sidewinder combination, could not be tempted into combat.

Over the following four days, the British air units were fully involved in aiding the 3rd Commando Brigade and the 5th Infantry Brigade to reach their curved start line for the attack on Port Stanley which was thought likely to end the campaign in a complete British victory. On 12 June the men of 3 Para fought a costly little action for Mount Longdon toward the northern end of the front, and just to their right the men of 2 Para moved forward to Wireless Ridge. On the southern end of the front 1 Welsh Guards and No. 42 Commando held Mount Harriet, and in the centre of the line No. 45 Commando and 22 SAS occupied Two Sisters and Murrel Heights respectively.

The improved weather now meant that more sorties could be undertaken by the Harrier close-support warplanes of the RAF, despite the temporary incapacitation of the forward operating base on 8 June by a Harrier's heavy landing. The campaign's first use of a laser-guided bomb

on 10 June was not successful as a result of problems in laser-designating the Argentine strongpoint that was the intended target.

As final preparations for the assault were coming together, on 12 June the destroyer *Glamorgan* was in the act of providing naval gunfire support for the troops when she was badly damaged by an MM.38 Exocet missile, the land-launched counterpart of the AM.39 Exocet air-launched anti-ship missile, in the process having her Wessex HAS.Mk 3 helicopter destroyed.

A short time after this Port Stanley reverberated to the detonation of air-burst bombs dropped by a Vulcan in the final 'Black Buck 7' raid of the series. Later in the same day, one Wessex HU.Mk 5 helicopter of No. 845 Squadron was involved in a daring raid against the Town Hall in Port Stanley. It was believed that a conference of the senior Argentine commanders in the Islands was taking place in the Town Hall. The mission was very nearly accomplished, except that one of the AS.12 wire-guided air-to-surface missiles fired by the Wessex struck the police station next to the Town Hall and the other failed to score a hit.

Enterprising attacks of an unconventional nature were not the sole preserve of the British, however, for on the following day A-4B warplanes of the *Grupo 5 de Caza* mounted an attack on the headquarters of the 3rd Commando Brigade on Mount Kent. Two four-aircraft flights were at readiness on the base at San Julian, to which it had moved from Rio Gallegos, and were launched on *Grupo 5's* only close support mission of the war.

In overall terms, the 48 Skyhawk warplanes (26 A-4B, 12 A-4C and 10 A-4Q machines) committed to the Falklands war had achieved creditable successes but only at severe cost: the aircraft had destroyed one destroyer, two frigates, one landing ship and one landing craft, but in the process lost 22 of their own number. These losses comprised eight to the Sea Harrier, seven to ship-launched surface-to-air missiles, four to ground-launched surface-to-air missiles and anti-aircraft fire (the latter including one to 'friendly' fire), and three to collision with the ground or the sea.

This A-4B of *Grupo 5,* flown by Teniente Araras, was photographed while taking on fuel on its way to attack the British forces landing near Fitzroy on 8 June. Later in the sortie C-226 was shot down over Choiseul Sound by an AIM-9L Sidewinder air-to-air missile from the Sea Harrier FRS.Mk 1 flown by Flight Lieutenant Morgan of No. 800 Squadron. Araras was killed

C-212 was an A-4B of *Grupo 5* flown by Teniente Luis Cervera on 13 June in Argentina's last Skyhawk mission of the Falklands war. In the course of his sortie, Cervera nearly shot down a Sea King HC.Mk 4 helicopter of No. 846 Squadron

Only four of the Skyhawk pilots made successful ejections, largely as a result of the very low altitude at which the aircraft operated. The attack achieved no significant result, and most of the Skyhawk attack aircraft suffered a measure of damage to ground fire even though all of the machines managed to regain their base. The day also saw the campaign's final Argentine bombing raid when at 22.55 hours a Canberra B.Mk 62 of *Grupo 2 de Bombardeo* was shot down over Mount Kent by a Sea Dart surface-to-air missile from the destroyer *Exeter*.

On 12 and 13 June there was some of the nastiest ground combat of the war as 2 Para, supported by Scout helicopters with AS.11 missiles, fought for Wireless Ridge in the north. Farther to the south, soldiers of 2 Scots and 1 Welsh Guards and 1/7 Gurkhas were lifted onto Mount Harriet by helicopters as the start point of their assault on Tumbledown Mountain. Comparatively lavish air support was available for this final effort, and at about 12.00 hours Harrier warplanes achieved the first successful attack of the campaign with a laser-guided bomb when an Argentine company headquarters position on Tumbledown, laser-designated by a ground-based forward air controller, was destroyed; an attack slightly later in the day also met with success when it destroyed an Argentine 105-mm (4.13-in) gun at Moody Brook. Fighting around Tumbledown Mountain continued to 14 June.

Port Stanley and the small area of land around it were now entirely isolated by British troops to the west and by sea to the north, east and south. During the middle of the day the *Hermes* launched two Harrier warplanes to undertake a laser-guided bomb attack on Sapper Hill, just to the south-west of Port Stanley, but just before beginning their attacks were called off when it was reported that white flags were starting to appear in Port Stanley. At 23.50 hours the Argentine commander signed the surrender document prepared by the British, formally ending the fighting that had in fact ceased early in the afternoon of 14 June.

The successful result of the war for the British was derived ultimately from the exercise of naval power supported by air power. This allowed the

task force to land high-quality ground forces on East Falkland at the right moment in the campaign, and then to support the ground forces' operations with naval gunfire and air attacks.

Right through the war the lines of communication and supply on which the British were wholly reliant were stretched to an extraordinary degree, and the sinking of just one transport, the admittedly large *Atlantic Conveyor* container ship, resulted in equipment shortages that revealed the slenderness of the logistic margins to which the British were operating. In purely naval terms the sinking of two destroyers, two frigates, an LSL and a container ship revealed much about the vulnerability of modern warship design and construction.

The British army's small force of Westland Scout AH.Mk 1 light turboshaft-powered helicopters was gainfully employed in the tactical reconnaissance, liaison, gunship and casualty evacuation roles

A decidedly war-weary HMS *Hermes* returns to Portsmouth after her involvement in the Falklands war

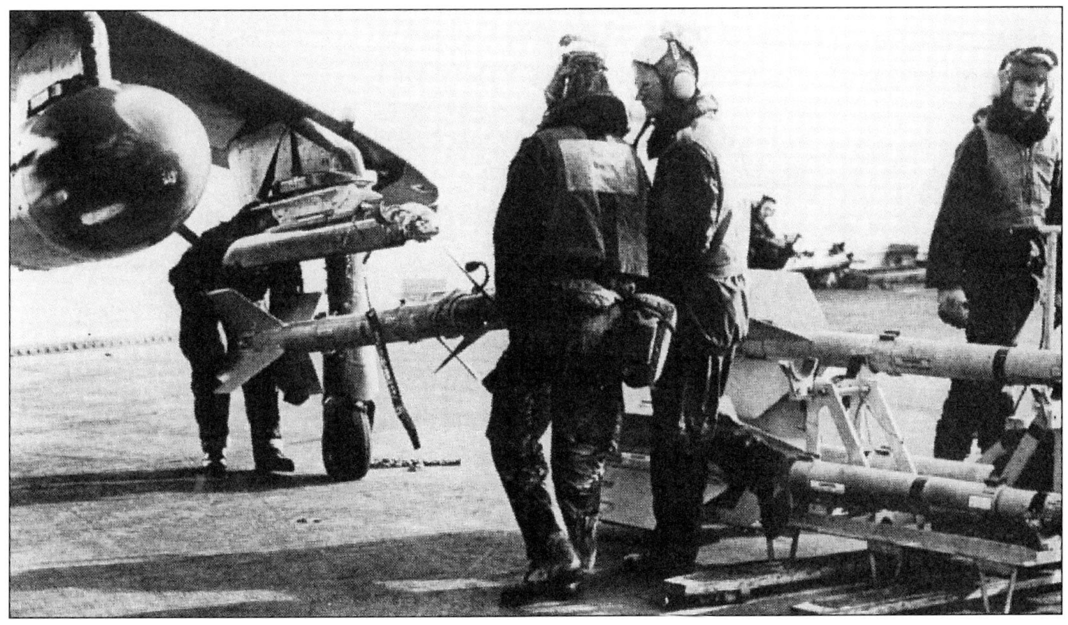

Armourers of No. 800 Squadron on board HMS *Hermes* prepare to load an AIM-9L Sidewinder short-range air-to-air missile onto the port underwing hardpoint of a Sea Harrier FRS.Mk 1

The carriers *Hermes* and *Invincible* exercised a determining part in the nature and progress of operations at sea and on land, for without the air power projected from these ships the landing in San Carlos Water and subsequent advance on Port Stanley could not have been undertaken. Completely vital air defence was provided by the Sea Harrier, despite the absence of any airborne early warning system that could otherwise have cued the fighters for superior tactical position. Between 1 May and 14 June the Sea Harrier fighters flew a total of 1,335 sorties, of which about 1,135 were combat air patrols, in the process firing 27 AIM-9L Sidewinder missiles of which 24 hit their targets, resulting in the destruction of 19 Argentine aircraft including 11 examples of the closely related Mirage IIIEA and Dagger supersonic fighters. The Sea Harriers also downed another six aircraft with 30-mm cannon fire.

In overall terms the members of the Harrier series proved themselves to be very reliable and also well able to cope with combat damage. As a result of the latter, few of the aircraft were lost to direct Argentine attack. The British surface-to-air missile systems, on which defence against Argentine air attack was largely reliant, were generally less capable, largely as a result of the difficulty of firing at low angles of elevation when there were friendly ships in the area: the Sea Dart missile destroyed seven aircraft and the Seawolf missile another three machines and, possibly, an Exocet missile. The land-based Rapier and the shoulder-launched Stinger and Blowpipe each destroyed one aeroplane.

The Falklands war also confirmed to the British the importance of the helicopter for a wide assortment of roles. This was nowhere more evident than in the aftermath of the loss of the *Atlantic Conveyor* together with three of the four heavy-lift Chinook twin-rotor helicopters allocated to the campaign, complete with all the spares, special tools and manuals etc. The loss meant that the one such machine already in the theatre had to struggle on alone, performing wonders of transports under the most adverse of conditions and without any possibility of spares and proper

With its ability to carry a large and/or weighty load in its hold or as a slung load, the Chinook HC.Mk 1 was a cornerstone of the British plan for the land campaign on East Falkland, so the loss of three out of the four allocated helicopters on the *Atlantic Conveyor* was a major blow

maintenance. It was fortunate for the British that they had available an effective medium-lift helicopter in the Sea King, which had not been designed for the role and, with the exception of the Sea King HC.Mk 4 variant, was scarcely optimised for the task. In the event, the Sea King helicopter force amassed more than 4,600 hours in the air during the campaign, in which the type was operated in a large number of tasks including casualty evacuation (more than 400 flights within a total of 2,253 sorties from 1 May).

Given the threat posed by the Argentine navy's submarine force, it was very fortunate that the ships of the task force had available for their protection two full squadrons of Sea King anti-submarine helicopters, which could be – and later were – diverted to other tasks, and were also supported by numbers of Lynx, Wasp and Wessex helicopters of various ship's flights.

As the Falklands war was fought at a distance very far from facilities of any type for support of equipment of all types, and of larger aircraft in particular, the Royal Air Force relied heavily on its inflight-refuelling capability over the two halves of the British lines of communication, namely the segments between the United Kingdom and Ascension Island, and between Ascension Island and the Falkland Islands.

During the conflict Vulcan bombers on the verge of final retirement were hastily revised with an inflight-refuelling probe, and similar adaptations for the Hercules transport and Nimrod maritime patrol types were designed, created and installed in time frames that would have been

With armourers in the foreground preparing to load bombs onto a Harrier GR.Mk 1 warplane, the British task force's sole surviving Chinook HC.Mk 1 (ZA718) of No. 18 Squadron, generally known as 'Bravo November', lands a slung load of freight on the port rear corner of the carrier HMS *Hermes'* flight deck

totally impossible under peacetime conditions. The task of refuelling British long-range aircraft fell on the Victor tankers of Nos. 55 and 57 Squadrons, which flew more than 600 sorties (only six of them aborted by equipment problems) in some 3,000 flying hours. An altogether different situation prevailed in the Fleet Air Arm, which lacked any inflight-refuelling capability and therefore had to scrub a number of missions where range was a critical factor.

The Hercules aircraft of the RAF's transport forces amassed some 13,000 flying hours that included, after 16 May, a total of 44 inflight-

Long-range sorties to and from the Falkland Islands from Ascension Island would have been impossible without the Victor K.Mk 2 tankers of Nos. 55 and 57 Squadrons. A typical 'Black Buck' mission required 10 tanker sorties (for five Vulcan refuellings) on the outward leg and two or three sorties (for one Vulcan refuelling) on the return leg

refuelled paradrops to the task force. The Nimrod aircraft recorded 111 sorties, many of them at extremely long range. The RAF's Harrier close-support warplanes, which needed inflight-refuelling to reach the *Hermes* from Ascension Island, flew 126 sorties in some 3½ weeks.

From the time that the government of Margaret Thatcher decided to resist the Argentine occupation of the Falkland Islands, extraordinary capability was revealed in the design, evaluation, manufacture or extemporisation, and installation of additional 'kit' on a host of aircraft types: the Nimrod, for example, was revised with an inflight-refuelling probe and provision for American-supplied weapons such as the AIM-9L Sidewinder air-to-air missile for self-protection and the AGM-84 Harpoon anti-ship missile for the offensive role.

With hindsight it is clear that the Argentine junta's decision to try to wrest the Falkland Islands from the United Kingdom was based on political rather than military thinking, possibly swayed by the fact that any attempt to retake the islands would have to travel some 8,000 miles (12,875 km) from the United Kingdom and be supported over that range. The British nonetheless opted to fight, and the campaign revealed, even without taking into account the morale and training deficiencies of the Argentine forces, that the bulk of the equipment used by the Argentine forces was decidedly inferior to that mustered against it by the British.

For the most part, Argentina's warplanes were obsolescent, and spares were in very short supply. The nature of the campaign, especially after the withdrawal of the *Veinticinco de Mayo,* meant that the aircraft had to operate at extreme range, without any effective electronic counter-measures systems, and generally without defensive armament so that the

Flown out to Ascension Island with the aid of multiple link-ups for inflight refuelling, this Harrier GR.Mk 1 is being readied for the short flight onto the *Atlantic Conveyor* and the journey through the South Atlantic to the vicinity of the Falkland Islands

The Twin Otter was one of five miscellaneous transport types operated from Comodoro Rivadavia by the FAA's *Grupo 9* for the transport role. Argentina received seven Twin Otter Mk 200 aircraft from de Havilland Canada in 1968-69, and the primary tasks of these aircraft were transport in the hands of LADE (the Argentine air force's airline). T-87 was written off in August 1977, but the other six machines (T-81 to T-86) were still in service

The CANA's counterpart to the Fleet Air Arm's Westland Sea King anti-submarine helicopter was the Sikorsky S-61D-4 Sea King. An initial four helicopters were delivered for purely naval use, while a fifth machine was completed with a VIP interior. H-31 (more properly 4-H-31) was the first purely naval helicopter, and in the Falklands war was operated by the 2 *Escuadrilla de Helicópteros* for shipborne and land-based service

maximum offensive load could be carried; this last factor was exacerbated by frequent weapons failures. Even so, and regardless of a strongly accelerating loss rate, Argentine pilots revealed themselves to be very courageous and skilful in continuing to press their attacks, in the process gaining notable successes against modern warships. Moreover, both military and civilian crews continued to fly transport aircraft into and out of BAM Malvinas at Port Stanley into the last stages of the war, although generally at night. The combat aircraft of the FAA logged a total of 2,782 flying hours, transport aircraft 7,719 flying hours and others, including civilian aircraft, 1,953 flying hours. The service planned 505 combat sorties, of which 445 were despatched but only 280 reached their targets.

APPENDICES

APPENDIX 1

THE FALKLANDS WAR: ARGENTINE ORDER OF BATTLE

Unit	*Aircraft type*	*Base*	*Task*	*Dates*
Comando de la Aviación Naval Argentina				
2 *Escuadrilla de Helicópteros*	S-61D-4	Bahia Blanca, Almirante Irizar, *Veinticinco de Mayo* and Rio Grande	Transport and ASW	00/03/82 to 14/06/82
Escuadrilla Anti-Submarina	S-2E	*Veinticinco de Mayo,* Bahia Blanca and Port Stanley	ASW and maritime recce	29/03/82 to 14/06/82
Escuadrilla de Exploración	SP-2H	Bahia Blanca and Rio Grande	Maritime recce	00/04/82 to 15/05/82
1 *Escuadrilla de Sostén Logistico Móvil*	Electra	Rio Grande	Transport	02/04/82 to 30/04/82
2 *Escuadrilla de Sostén Logìstico Móvil*	F.28-3000M	Rio Grande	Transport	02/04/82 to 30/04/82
1 *Escuadrilla de Ataque*	MB-326GB and MB-339A	Almirante Zar, Bahia Blanca, Rio Grande and Port Stanley	Ground attack	02/04/82 to 23/04/82
4 *Escuadrilla de Ataque*	T-34C-1	Punta del Indio, Rio Grande, Port Stanley and Pebble Island	Ground attack	15/04/82 to 23/04/82
2 *Escuadrilla de Caza y Ataque*	Super Etendard	Bahia Blanca and Rio Grande	Anti-ship attack	19/04/82 to 30/05/82
1 *Escuadrilla de Helicopteros*	Lynx Mk 23 and Alouette III	various ships	ASW and liaison	25/03/82 to 19/06/82
3 *Escuadrilla de Caza y Ataque*	A-4Q	*Veinticinco de Mayo* and Bahia Blanca	Ground and anti-ship attack	28/03/82 to 14/06/82
Prefectura Naval Argentina	Skyvan & Puma	Port Stanley and Pebble Island	Transport and communications	01/04/82 to 15/05/82
Comando de Aviación del Ejército				
Batallón de Aviación de Combate 601	A 109A, UH-1H, Puma and CH-47C	various on Falklands	Transport, gunship and liaison	23/03/82 to 17/06/82

Unit	*Aircraft type*	*Base*	*Task*	*Dates*
Fuerza Aérea Argentina				
I Escuadrón, Grupo Aérofotográfico	Learjet 35A	Comodoro Rivadavia, Almirante Zar and Rio Gallegos	Recce	00/04/82 to 14/06/82
I Escuadrón, Grupo Aereo 1 de Transporte	C-130E/H and KC-130H	Comodoro Rivadavia	Transport, recce and tanking	01/04/82 to 14/06/82
Grupo Aereo 9 de Transporte	F.27-400/500/600, F.28-1000, Twin Otter Mk 200, One-Eleven and Model 707-300	Comodoro Rivadavia	Transport	02/04/82 to 29/05/82
Grupo 3 de Ataque	IA-58 Pucará	Santa Cruz, Port Stanley, Goose Green and Pebble Island	Attack	02/04/82 to 13/06/82
Grupo 16 de Caza	CH-47C and Model 212	various in Argentina and Port Stanley	SAR, recce and transport	07/04/82 to 14/06/82
Grupo 4 de Caza	A-4C	San Julian	Ground and anti-ship attack	11/04/82 to 08/06/82
Grupo 5 de Caza	A-4B	Rio Gallegos	Ground and anti-ship attack	14/04/82 to 14/06/82
Escuadrón II, Grupo 1 de Transporte Militar	Model 707	Comodoro Rivadavia, El Palomar and Ezeiza	Transport and recce	20/04/82 to 07/06/82
Escuadrón II, Grupo 6 de Caza	Dagger	San Julian	Air defence and escort	25/04/82 to 13/06/82
Escuadrón Fenix	various	various in Argentina	communications, SAR and pathfinding	27/04/82 to 14/06/82
Grupo 8 de Caza	Mirage IIIEA	Comodoro Rivadavia and Rio Gallegos	Air defence & escort	01/05/82 to 14/06/82
Grupo 2 de Bombardeo	Canberra B.Mk 62	Almirante Zar and Rio Gallegos	Bombing	01/05/82 to 14/06/82

APPENDIX 2

THE FALKLANDS WAR: BRITISH ORDER OF BATTLE

Unit	*Aircraft type*	*Base*	*Task*	*Dates*
Royal Air Force				
No. 51 Sqn	Nimrod R.Mk 1	Ascension (possibly Chile)	Elint	00/04/82 to 00/06/82
No. 39 Sqn	Canberra PR.Mk 9	Punta Arenas (?)	Photo-recce	00/04/82 to 00/06/82
No. 24 Sqn	Hercules C.Mks 1/3	Ascension and Stanley	Transport	02/04/82 to 19/08/83
No. 30 Sqn	Hercules C.Mks 1/3	Ascension and Stanley	Transport	02/04/82 to 19/08/83
No. 47 Sqn	Hercules C.Mks 1/3	Ascension and Stanley	Transport	02/04/82 to 19/08/83
No. 70 Sqn	Hercules C.Mks 1/3	Ascension and Stanley	Transport	02/04/82 to 19/08/83
No. 10 Sqn	VC10 C.Mk 1	Ascension and Stanley	Transport	03/04/82 to 31/07/82
No. 18 Sqn	Chinook HC.Mk 1	Ascension and Port San Carlos	Transport	06/04/82 to 19/10/83
No. 42 Sqn	Nimrod MR.Mk 1	Ascension	Recce	06/04/82 to 05/11/82
No. 120 Sqn	Nimrod MR.Mk 2	Ascension	Recce	13/04/82 to 19/08/82
No. 201 Sqn	Nimrod MR.Mk 2	Ascension	Recce	13/04/82 to 19/08/82
No. 206 Sqn	Nimrod MR.Mk 2	Ascension	Recce	13/04/82 to 19/08/82
No. 55 Sqn	Victor K.Mk 2	Ascension and Stanley	Tanking	18/04/82 to 12/03/85
No. 57 Sqn	Victor K.Mk 2	Ascension and Stanley	Tanking	18/04/82 to 12/03/85
No. 44 Sqn	Vulcan B.Mk 2	Ascension	Bombing	19/04/82 to 14/06/82
No. 50 Sqn	Vulcan B.Mk 2	Ascension	Bombing	19/04/82 to 14/06/82
No. 101 Sqn	Vulcan B.Mk 2	Ascension	Bombing	19/04/82 to 14/06/82
No. 1 Sqn	Harrier GR.Mk 3	Ascension, *Hermes* and Stanley	Ground attack	03/05/82 to 10/11/82
No. 202 Sqn	Sea King HAR.Mk 3	Ascension	Transport	09/05/82 to 07/09/82
No. 29 Sqn	Phantom FGR.Mk 2	Ascension	Air defence	25/05/82 to 14/07/82
Fleet Air Arm				
No. 800 Sqn	Sea Harrier FRS.Mk 1	*Hermes*, Port San Carlos and Stanley	Air defence and ground attack	05/04/82 to 03/07/82
No. 801 Sqn	Sea Harrier FRS.Mk 1	*Invincible*, Port San Carlos and Stanley	Air defence and ground attack	05/04/82 to 28/08/82
No. 809 Sqn	Sea Harrier FRS.Mk 1	*Hermes* and *Invincible*	Air defence and ground attack	18/05/82 to 21/10/82
No. 820 Sqn	Sea King HAS.Mk 5	*Invincible*, Ascension and Stanley	Transport, ASW and SAR	05/04/82 to 28/08/82
No. 824 Sqn (A Flight)	Sea King HAS.Mk 2A	*Olmeda* and Port San Carlos	ASW and transport	05/04/82 to 21/06/82
No. 824 Sqn (C flight)	Sea King HAS.Mk 2A	*Fort Grange*	ASW and transport	03/06/82 to 17/09/82
No. 825 Sqn	Sea King HAS.Mk 2/2A	*Queen Elizabeth 2*, *Atlantic Causeway* and Port San Carlos	Transport	27/05/82 to 13/07/82

Unit	Aircraft type	Base	Task	Dates
No. 826 Sqn	Sea King HAS. Mk 5	*Hermes* and Port San Carlos	ASW, SAR and casevac	05/04/82 to 03/07/82
No. 846 Sqn	Sea King HC.Mk 4	*Hermes, Fearless, Intrepid, Canberra, Elk, Norland* & various on Falklands	Transport	05/04/82 to 02/07/82
No. 737 Sqn	Wessex HAS.Mk 3	*Antrim* and *Glamorgan*	ASW, transport and casevac	14/04/82 to 28/06/82
No. 845 Sqn (A Flight)	Wessex HU.Mk 5	*Resource* and Stanley	Transport	30/04/82 to 26/06/82
No. 845 Sqn (B Flight)	Wessex HU.Mk 5	*Fort Austin,* Port San Carlos and Stanley	Transport	03/05/82 to 03/07/82
No. 845 Sqn (C Flight)	Wessex HU.Mk 5	*Tidespring* and Port San Carlos	Transport	21/04/82 to 03/07/82
No. 845 Sqn (D Flight)	Wessex HU.Mk 5	Ascension	Transport	11/04/82 to 00/10/82
No. 845 Sqn (E Flight)	Wessex HU.Mk 5	*Tidepool* and various on Falklands	Transport and casevac	05/05/82 to 12/07/82
No. 847 Sqn	Wessex HU.Mk 5	*Engadine, Atlantic Causeway,* Port San Carlos and various on Falklands	Transport and casevac	01/06/82 to 10/07/82
No. 848 Sqn (A Flight)	Wessex HU.Mk 5	*Endurance* and *Regent*	Transport	01/05/82 to 10/07/82
No. 848 Sqn (B Flight)	Wessex HU.Mk 5	*Olna* and Port San Carlos	Transport	30/05/82 to 31/08/82
No. 848 Sqn (C Flight)	Wessex HU.Mk 5	*Fort Austin* and *Olwen*	Transport	28/06/82 to 16/10/82
No. 848 Sqn (D Flight)	Wessex HU.Mk 5	*Atlantic Conveyor* and *Astronomer*	Transport	18/05/82 to 25/05/82
No. 815 Sqn	Lynx HAS.Mk 2	'Sheffield', 'Broadsword' and 'Amazon' classes	ASW, electronic warfare and vertrep	27/06/82 to 02/09/82
No. 829 Sqn	Wasp HAS.Mk 1	'Leander' and 'Rothesay' classes	ASW, liaison and vertrep	27/06/82 to 02/09/82

Unit	Aircraft type	Base	Task	Dates
Royal Marines				
3rd Commando Brigade Air Sqn	Scout AH.Mk 1 and Gazelle AH.Mk 1	various on Falklands	Recce, liaison, gunship and casevac	16/05/82 to 22/06/82
Army Air Corps				
No. 656 Sqn	Scout AH.Mk 1 and Gazelle AH.Mk 1	various on Falklands	Recce, liaison, gunship and casevac	19/05/82 to 02/08/82

APPENDIX 3

AIR-CAPABLE BRITISH SHIPS IN THE FALKLANDS TASK FORCE

Aircraft carriers

'Hermes' class (HMS *Hermes,* entered operational area 25/4/82)
Displacement: 28,700 tons
Maximum speed: 28 kt
Complement: 1,350
Aircraft: 12 Sea Harrier FRS.Mk 1 and 18 Sea King
Anti-aircraft defence: two GWS-22 Seacat short-range quadruple SAM launchers

'Invincible' class (HMS *Invincible* 25/4/82)
Displacement: 19,810 tons
Maximum speed: 28 kt
Complement: 1,000
Aircraft: eight Sea Harrier FRS.Mk 1 and 15 Sea King
Anti-aircraft defence: two Sea Dart medium-range SAM launchers

Destroyers and frigates

'Type 82' class (HMS *Bristol* 23/5/82)
Displacement: 7,100 tons
Maximum speed: 29 kt
Complement: 407
Aircraft: one Wasp HAS.Mk 1
Anti-aircraft defence: one 4.5-in (114-mm) DP gun and two 20-mm cannon

'County' class (HMS *Antrim* 17/4/82 and HMS *Glamorgan* 25/4/82)
Displacement: 6,200 tons
Maximum speed: 30 kt
Complement: 471
Aircraft: one Wessex HAS.Mk 3
Anti-aircraft defence: two Seaslug Mk 2 medium-range SAM launchers, two GWS-22 Seacat short-range quadruple SAM launchers and two 4.5-in (114-mm) DP guns

'Type 42' class (HMS *Cardiff* 23/5/82, HMS *Coventry* 20/4/82, HMS Exeter 19/5/82, HMS *Glasgow* 20/4/82 and HMS *Sheffield* 20/4/82)
Displacement: 4,100 tons
Maximum speed: 29 kt
Complement: 268
Aircraft: one Lynx HAS.Mk 2
Anti-aircraft defence: two Sea Dart medium-range SAM launchers, one 4.5-in (114-mm) DP gun and two 20-mm cannon

'Type 22' class (HMS *Brilliant* 20/4/82 and HMS *Broadsword* 25/4/82)
Displacement: 4,000 tons
Maximum speed: 30 kt
Complement: 223
Aircraft: two Lynx HAS.Mk 2
Anti-aircraft defence: two Seawolf short-range sextuple SAM launchers and two 40-mm Bofors guns

'Type 21' class (HMS *Active* 23/5/82, HMS *Alacrity* 25/4/82, HMS *Ambuscade* 18/5/82, HMS *Antelope* 18/5/82, HMS *Ardent* 13/5/82, HMS *Arrow* 20/4/82 and HMS *Avenger* 23/5/82)
Displacement: 3,250 tons
Maximum speed: 30 kt
Complement: 235
Aircraft: one Lynx HAS.Mk 2
Anti-aircraft defence: one GWS-24 Seacat short-range quadruple SAM launcher, one 4.5-in (114-mm) DP gun and two 20-mm cannon

'Leander (Exocet)' class (HMS *Argonaut* 13/5/82, HMS *Penelope* 23/5/82 and HMS *Minerva* 23/5/82)
Displacement: 3,200 tons
Maximum speed: 28 kt
Complement: 223
Aircraft: one Wasp HAS.Mk 1 or Lynx HAS.Mk 2
Anti-aircraft defence: three GWS-22 Seacat short-range quadruple SAM launchers and one 40-mm Bofors gun

'Leander (Broad-beam)' class (HMS *Andromeda* 23/5/82)
Displacement: 2,960 tons
Maximum speed: 28
Complement: 260
Aircraft: one Lynx HAS.Mk 2
Anti-aircraft defence: two Seawolf short-range sextuple SAM launchers

'Rothesay' class (HMS *Yarmouth* 25/4/82 and HMS *Plymouth* 17/4/82)
Displacement: 2,800 tons
Maximum speed: 30 kt
Complement: 235
Aircraft: one Wasp HAS.Mk 1
Anti-aircraft defence: one GWS-20 Seacat short-range quadruple SAM launcher and two 4.5-in (114-mm) DP guns

Ice patrol ship

'Endurance' class (HMS *Endurance* 00/5/82)
Displacement: 3,600 tons
Maximum speed: 14.5 kt
Complement: 119
Aircraft: two Wasp HAS.Mk 1
Anti-aircraft defence: two 20-mm cannon

Assault ships

'Fearless' class (HMS *Fearless* 13/5/82 and HMS *Intrepid* 13/5/82)
Displacement: 5,675 tons
Maximum speed: 21 kt
Complement: 580 plus provision for 400/700 troops for extended/short periods
Aircraft: five Wessex HU.Mk 5 or four Sea King HC.Mk 4
Anti-aircraft defence: four GWS-20 Seacat short-range quadruple SAM launchers and two 40-mm Bofors guns

Landing ships logistic

'Sir Bedivere' class (RFA-manned RFA *Sir Bedivere* 18/5/82, RFA *Sir Galahad* 8/5/82, RFA *Sir Geraint* 8/5/82, RFA *Sir Percivale* 8/5/82, RFA *Sir Tristram* 8/5/82 and RFA *Sir Lancelot* 8/5/82)
Displacement: 5,675 tons
Maximum speed: 17 kt
Complement: 68 plus provision for 340/534 troops for extended/short periods
Aircraft: facilities for helicopter operations and storage for nine helicopters
Anti-aircraft defence: two 40-mm Bofors guns

Troop transport, equipment ferry and other support ships of the Royal Fleet Auxiliary and Ships Taken Up From Trade

Queen Elizabeth 2 (23/5/82 and 67,000 tons with facilities for helicopter operations)
Canberra (13/5/82 and 44,810 tons with facilities for helicopter operations)
Atlantic Causeway (25/5/82 and 14,945 tons with facilities for STOVL aircraft and helicopter operations)
Atlantic Conveyor (13/5/82 and 14,945 tons with facilities for STOVL aircraft and helicopter operations)
RFA *Fort Austin* (26/4/82 and 23,600 tons with facilities for up to four Sea King)
RFA *Fort Grange* (26/5/82 and 23,600 tons with facilities for up to four Sea King)
RFA *Resource* (25/4/82 and 22,890 tons with facilities for up to four Sea King)
RFA *Regent* (8/5/82 and 22,890 tons with facilities for up to four Sea King)
RFA *Stromness* (13/5/82 and 16,790 tons with facilities for one Sea King)
HMS *Hydra* (14/5/82 and 2,745 tons with facilities for one Wasp HAS.Mk 1)
HMS *Herald* (15/5/82 and 2,945 tons with facilities for one Wasp HAS.Mk 1)
HMS *Hecla* (9/5/82 and 2,745 tons with facilities for one Wasp HAS.Mk 1)
HMS *Engadine* (2/6/82 and 9,000 tons with four Wessex HU.Mk 5 or two Wasp HAS.Mk 1 and two Sea King)
RFA *Olmeda* (25/4/82 and 36,000 tons with facilities for four Sea King)
RFA *Olna* (23/5/82 and 36,000 tons with facilities for four Sea King)
RFA *Tidespring* (17/4/82 and 27,400 tons wth facilities for four Sea King)
RFA *Tidepool* (13/5/82 and 27,400 tons with facilities for four Sea King)
RFA *Blue Rover* (2/5/82 and 11,520 tons with facilities for one Sea King)

APPENDIX 4

ARGENTINE LOSSES

A-4 Skyhawk

Date	*Aeroplane*	*Unit*	*Circumstances*
9 May	A-4C (C-313)	*Grupo 4*	Crashed into high ground on South Jason Island, north-west of West Falkland, Teniente Casco being killed
9 May	A-4C (C-303)	*Grupo 4*	Crashed into the sea in bad visibility near South Jason Island, north-west of West Falkland, Teniente Farias being killed
12 May	A-4B (C-246)	*Grupo 5*	Downed by a Seawolf SAM from HMS *Brilliant* off Port Stanley, Primer Teniente Bustos being killed
12 May	A-4B (C-208)	*Grupo 5*	Downed by a Seawolf SAM from HMS *Brilliant* off Port Stanley, Teniente Ibarlucea being killed
12 May	A-4B (C-206)	*Grupo 5*	Crashed into the sea off Port Stanley while attacking HMS *Glasgow* and HMS *Brilliant* during evasive manoeuvring to avoid Seawolf SAMs, Teniente Nivoli being killed
12 May	A-4B (C-248)	*Grupo 5*	Downed in error by Argentine 35-mm AA fire over Goose Green, Primer Teniente Gavazzi being killed
21 May	A-4C (C-325)	*Grupo 4*	Downed over West Falkland by Sea Harrier of No. 800 Sqn flown by Lieutenant Commander Blissett, Primer Teniente Manzotti being killed
21 May	A-4C (C-309)	*Grupo 4*	Downed over West Falkland by Sea Harrier of No. 800 Sqn flown by Lieutenant Commander Thomas, Teniente Lopez being killed
21 May	A-4Q (3-A-307, 0660)	3 *Escuadrilla*	Downed over Falkland Sound by AIM-9L from a Sea Harrier of No. 800 Sqn flown by Lieutenant Morrell after attacking HMS *Ardent*, Capitán de Corbeta Philippi ejecting
21 May	A-4Q (3-A-314, 0667)	3 *Escuadrilla*	Downed over Falkland Sound by cannon fire from a Sea Harrier of No. 800 Sqn flown by Flight Lieutenant Leeming, Teniente de Fregata Marquez being killed
21 May	A-4Q (3-A-312, 0665)	3 *Escuadrilla*	Damaged over Falkland Sound by cannon fire from a Sea Harrier flown by Lieutenant Morrell, Teniente de Navio Arca attempting to land at Port Stanley but landing gear damage then forcing him to bale out as the Skyhawk continued to fly on and being downed by Argentine AA fire
23 May	A-4B (C-242)	*Grupo 5*	Downed by SAM, AA and small arms fire over San Carlos Water while attacking HMS *Antelope*, Primer Teniente Guadagnini being killed
23 May	A-4Q (3-A-306, 0659)	3 *Escuadrilla*	Bombs hung up during attack on HMS *Antelope*, and on return to Rio Grande Capitán de Corbeta Zubizarreta attempted to land but veered off the icy runway after failing to engage the emergency arresting gear, the pilot then ejecting but his seat failing to work properly leading to injuries from which he died; damage to the Skyhawk was light
24 May	A-4C (C-305)	*Grupo 4*	Downed by AA fire and crashed in King George Bay, West Falkland, Teniente Bono being killed
25 May	A-4B (C-244)	*Grupo 5*	Downed by Sea Dart SAM from HMS *Coventry* north of Pebble Island, Capitán Palaver being killed
25 May	A-4C (C-319)	*Grupo 4*	Downed over San Carlos Water by AA fire and Rapier SAM, Teniente Lucero ejecting
25 May	A-4C (C-304)	*Grupo 4*	Downed by Sea Dart SAM from HMS *Coventry* north of Pebble Island, Capitán Garcia ejecting but later dying of exposure
27 May	A-4B (C-215)	*Grupo 5*	Downed by 40-mm Bofors AA fire from HMS *Fearless* after successfully attacking British positions at Ajax Bay, Primer Teniente Velasco ejecting near Port Howard, West Falkland
30 May	A-4C (C-301)	*Grupo 4*	Downed east of the Falkland Islands by Sea Dart SAM from HMS *Exeter*, Primer Teniente Vazquez being killed
30 May	A-4C (C-310)	*Grupo 4*	Downed east of the Falkland Islands by Sea Dart SAM from HMS *Exeter*, Primer Teniente being killed
8 June	A-4B (C-226)	*Grupo 5*	Downed over Choiseul Sound by a Sea Harrier of No. 800 Sqn flown by Flight Lieutenant Morgan, Teniente Arraras being killed
8 June	A-4B (C-228)	*Grupo 5*	Downed over Choiseul Sound, just after scoring a bomb hit on the land-

			ing craft *Foxtrot-4* from HMS *Fearless*, by a Sea Harrier of No. 800 Sqn flown by Flight Lieutenant Morgan, Alferez Vazquez ejecting but being killed
8 June	A-4B (C-204)	*Grupo 5*	Downed by a Sea Harrier of No. 800 Sqn flown by Lieutenant Smith over Choiseul Sound, Primer Teniente Bolzan being killed

Canberra

Date	*Aeroplane*	*Unit*	*Circumstances*
1 May	Canberra B.Mk 62 (B-110)	*Grupo 2*	Downed, while trying to find HMS *Invincible*, by an AIM-9L Sidewinder from a Sea Harrier of No. 801 Squadron flown by Lieutenant Curtis, Teniente de Ibañez and Primer Teniente Gonzalez ejecting but never being found
13 June	Canberra B.Mk 62 (B-108)	*Grupo 2*	Downed near Lively Island by a Sea Dart SAM from HMS *Exeter*, Capitán Pastan ejecting but Capitán Casado being trapped in the aeroplane and killed

Dagger and Mirage IIIEA

Date	*Aeroplane*	*Unit*	*Circumstances*
1 May	Mirage IIIEA (I-105)	*Grupo 8*	Downed over Pebble Island by an AIM-9L AAM from a Sea Harrier of No. 801 Sqn flown by Flight Lieutenant Barton, Primer Teniente Perona being killed
1 May	Mirage IIIEA (I-109)	*Grupo 8*	Damaged near Port Stanley by a Sea Harrier of No. 801 Sqn flown by Lieutenant Thomas and then shot down by Argentine 35-mm AA fire while attempting to make an emergency landing at Port Stanley, Capitán Garcia Cuerva being killed
1 May	Dagger (C-433)	*Grupo 6*	Downed over Lively Island by an AIM-9L AAM from a Sea Harrier of No. 800 Sqn flown by Lieutenant Penfold, Primer Teniente Ardiles being killed
21 May	Dagger (C-428)	*Grupo 6*	Downed over San Carlos Water by a Seawolf SAM probably fired by HMS *Broadsword*, Teniente Bean being killed
21 May	Dagger (C-409)	*Grupo 6*	Downed over West Falkland by an AIM-9L AAM from a Sea Harrier of No. 800 Sqn flown by Lieutenant Commander Frederiksen, Primer Teniente Luna ejecting
21 May	Dagger (C-404)	*Grupo 6*	Downed over West Falkland by an AIM-9L AAM from a Sea Harrier of No. 800 Sqn flown by Lieutenant Thomas, Mayor Piuma ejecting
21 May	Dagger (C-403)	*Grupo 6*	Downed over West Falkland by an AIM-9L AAM from a Sea Harrier of No. 800 Sqn flown by Lieutenant Thomas, Capitán Donadille ejecting
21 May	Dagger (C-407)	*Grupo 6*	Downed over West Falkland by an AIM-9L AAM from a Sea Harrier of No. 800 Sqn flown by Lieutenant Commander Ward, Primer Teniente Senn ejecting
23 May	Dagger (C-437)	*Grupo 6*	Downed near Pebble Island by an AIM-9L from a Sea Harrier of No. 800 Sqn flown by Lieutenant Hale, Teniente Volponi being killed
24 May	Dagger (C-419)	*Grupo 6*	Downed near Pebble Island by an AIM-9L AAM from a Sea Harrier of No. 800 Sqn flown by Lieutenant Commander Auld, Mayor Puga ejecting
24 May	Dagger (C-430)	*Grupo 6*	Downed near Pebble Island by an AIM-9L AAM from a Sea Harrier of No. 800 Sqn flown by Lieutenant Commander Auld, Capitán Diaz ejecting
24 May	Dagger (C-410)	*Grupo 6*	Downed over Pebble Island by an AIM-9L AAM from a Sea Harrier of No. 800 Sqn flown by Lieutenant Smith, Teniente Castillo being killed
29 May	Dagger (C-436)	*Grupo 6*	Downed over San Carlos Water by a Rapier SAM, Teniente Berhardt being killed

COLOUR PLATES

1

BAe Harrier GR.Mk 3, Serial Number: XW767, No. 1 Squadron, Royal Air Force, HMS *Hermes*
XW767 operated from the carrier HMS *Hermes* before moving to improvised landing strips on East Falkland. The aeroplane was built within the context of the second production order for the Harrier (17 single- and three two-seat aircraft), and was completed to the initial Harrier GR.Mk 1 standard although it was later upgraded to Harrier GR.Mk 3 standard with changes including a revised and longer nose carrying a laser range-finder and marked-target seeker.

2

BAe Vulcan B.Mk 2A, Serial Number: XM597, No. 50 Squadron, Royal Air Force, Ascension Island
A long-range bomber of No. 50 Squadron, normally a unit of the Waddington Wing based at the base of that name in Lincolnshire. The squadron was one of three such units involved in the Falklands war, and was based at Wideawake Airfield on Ascension Island for attacks on the Argentine air installations just outside Port Stanley. Having undertaken the partially successful second 'Black Buck' mission against Argentine radar equipments, one of which was damaged by an AGM-45 Shrike missile on 31 May, the same aeroplane was used in the third attack during 3 June, which destroyed a Skyguard radar with the same type of missile. However, on its way back to Ascension Island, Squadron Leader Neil McDougall's Vulcan broke its flight-refuelling probe while attempting to link up with a Victor K.Mk 2 tanker. With insufficient fuel to return to base, McDougall had no alternative but to make an emergency landing at Rio de Janeiro airport in neutral Brazil, where the Vulcan and its crew were held for nine days before being allowed to leave.

3

BAe Victor K.Mk 2, Serial Number: XL188, No. 55 Squadron, Royal Air Force, Ascension Island
As indicated by the badge on the fin (a white circle carrying a blue motif of a forearm brandishing a spear), XL188 was a tanker of the RAF's No. 55 Squadron. This squadron was based at Wideawake Airfield on Ascension Island during the Falklands war, as too were similar aircraft of No. 57 Squadron and No. 232 Operational Conversion Unit. All three units' home base was RAF Marham in eastern England. Each of the aircraft operated with three hose and drum units: one built into the rear part of the lower fuselage and the other two as red/white-striped pods under the outer wing panels.

4

BAe Sea Harrier FRS.Mk 1, Serial Number: ZA174, No. 801 Squadron, Fleet Air Arm, HMS *Invincible*
Sea Harrier multi-role fighters of the Fleet Air Arm's No. 801 Squadron operated from HMS *Invincible* during the Falklands war. The aeroplane was the first of the 10 machines that constituted the second production batch of Sea Harrier FRS.Mk 1 warplanes delivered between November 1981 and January 1984.

5

Boeing Chinook HC.Mk 1, Serial Number: ZA718, No. 18 Squadron, Royal Air Force
ZA718 was the only one of four Boeing Chinook HC.Mk 1 helicopters of No. 18 Squadron (normally based at RAF Odiham in Hampshire) not to be lost with the container ship *Atlantic Conveyor*. As such 'Bravo November' became the only heavy-lift helicopter available to the British forces on the Falkland Islands and performed magnificently in this vital task.

6

Aermacchi MB-339A, Serial Number: 4-A-113, 1 Escuadrilla de Ataque, Comando de la Aviación Naval Argentina
4-A-113 was the fourth of 10 examples of the MB-339A which the CANA received from a time late in 1980 for service in the advanced flying and weapons training roles. The aircraft were allocated to the III Escuadra Naval's 1 Escuadrilla de Ataque at BAN Punta del Indio, where they partnered the survivors of eight Aermacchi MB-326GB trainers that had been procured to replace the service's aged Grumman F9F-2 Panther aircraft. During the Falklands war the MB-339A aircraft were used in the light attack role from three mainland bases (at Almirante Zar, Bahia Blanca and Rio Grande) as well as from Port Stanley in the Falklands, in the process losing five of their number.

7

Dassault Super Etendard, Serial Number: 3-A-201, 2 Escuadrilla de Caza y Ataque, Comando de la Aviación Naval Argentina
3-A-201 was the first of the five Dassault Super Etendard warplanes which the Argentine naval air command received before the Falklands war, the nine aircraft completing the service's order being delivered only after the end of hostilities. The five aircraft were operated by the 2 Escuadrilla de Caza y Ataque not from the carrier ARA *Veinticinco de Mayo* as planned, but rather from the shore bases at BAN Comandante Espora at Bahia Blanca and BAN Rio Grande. 3-A-201 was not used operationally during the Falklands war, being reserved as a source of spares to keep the other four aircraft serviceable.

8

McDonnell Douglas A-4Q Skyhawk, Serial Number: 3-A-304, 3 Escuadrilla de Caza y Ataque, Comando de la Aviación Naval Argentina
3-A-304 was the fourth of 16 McDonnell Douglas

A-4Q Skyhawk aircraft operated by the CANA's 3 Escuadrilla de Caza y Ataque for the ground-attack and anti-ship roles. The aircraft had been upgraded from A-4B standard by the manufacturer at Santa Monica, California, during the late 1960s and delivered for carrierborne service on the ARA *Veinticinco de Mayo.* In 1982 the carrier was quickly withdrawn to port, and the eight serviceable Skyhawk warplanes (supplemented by another two returned to operational capability during the conflict) then operated from BAM Comandante Espora at Bahia Blanca. This aeroplane was not one of the three Skyhawk warplanes (3-A-307, 3-A-312 and 3-A-314) that the CANA lost in the war to BAe Sea Harrier attacks.

9

FMA IA-58A Pucará, Serial Number: A-549, Grupo 3 de Ataque, Fuerza Aérea Argentina

A-549 was one of the second batch of FMA IA-58A Pucará light attack and counter-insurgency warplanes to be built in Argentina. The aeroplane was operated on the Falkland Islands by the Argentine Air Force's Grupo 3 de Ataque, whose main bases were at BAM Malvinas and BAM Condor (Port Stanley and Goose Green respectively), with some of the aircraft forward deployed to Santa Cruz and Pebble Island. Some 25 of the aircraft were destroyed during the course of the war, but A-549 survived to be taken by the British at the end of the campaign and shipped back to the UK for technical evaluation and display.

10

Dassault Mirage IIIEA, Serial Number: I-007, Grupo 8 de Caza, Fuerza Aérea Argentina

Carrying the fin badge of the Argentine Air Force's Grupo 8 de Caza, which operated from BAM Comodoro Rivadavia and BAM Rio Gallegos during the course of the Falklands war, this Dassault Mirage IIIEA (seen in 'clean' condition without the one centreline R.530 medium-range AAM and underwing combination of two R.550 Magic short-range AAMs and two drop tanks that were possible) was one of 17 such aircraft ordered by Argentina in August 1970 (two Mirage IIIDA two-seat as well as 10 Mirage IIIEA single-seat aircraft) and 1977 (seven Mirage IIIEA aircraft).

11

BAe Canberra B.Mk 62, Serial Number: B-101, Grupo 2 de Bombardeo, Fuerza Aérea Argentina

Delivered on 16 November 1970, B-101 was the first of 12 BAe Canberra warplanes received by the Argentine Air Force in response to an order of mid-1969 for 10 Canberra B.Mk 62 bombers and two Canberra T.Mk 64 trainers. In 1981 the service also ordered single examples of the two variants produced as conversions of ex-RAF B.Mk 2 and T.Mk 4 machines. In the Falklands war the Canberra bombers were operated by the Grupo 2 de Bombardeo operating from BAN Almirante Zar (located outside Trelew) and BAM Rio Gallegos on the Argentine mainland.

12

Grumman S-2E Tracker, Serial Number: 2-AS-26, Escuadrilla Anti-Submarina, Comando de la Aviación Naval Argentina

The Servicio de Aviación Naval (later the Comando de la Aviación Naval Argentina) originally received six examples of the Grumman S-2A Tracker in February 1962 for the anti-submarine role in the hands of the 1 Escuadrilla Anti-Submarina from the BAN Punto del Indio and BAN Comandante Espora shore bases, but later from the carrier ARA *Independencia* and then the ARA *Veinticinco de Mayo.* These six aircraft were supplemented from 1967 by a single S-2F that was lost to a ground fire in 1975. From January 1978 the surviving four aircraft were relegated to secondary tasks as their primary role was assumed by six examples of the more modern S-2E variant of the Tracker. During the Falklands war, the S-2E warplanes of what was now the Escuadrilla Anti-Submarina operated for a short time from the *Veinticinco de Mayo,* but mostly from the shore bases at Bahia Blanca (BAN Comandante Espora) and Port Stanley (BAM Malvinas) in the anti-submarine and maritime reconnaissance roles. The aeroplane illustrated, 2-AS-26, was the last of the six S-2E aircraft to be taken into Argentine service.

13

Learjet 35A, Serial Number: VR-17, I Escuadrón, Grupo Aérofotográfico, Fuerza Aérea Argentina

At the time of the Falklands war, the Argentine Air Force operated five examples of the Learjet 35A. The first two (delivered in 1977 with the serials T-21 and T-22) were used for communications and photo-survey, the second pair (delivered in 1980 with the serials T-23 and T-24) were operated in the nav-aid calibration role, and the last (delivered in 1981 with the serial VR-17) was used for radio calibration. This last machine was operated by the I Escuadrón, Grupo Aérofotográfico from the BAM Comodoro Rivadavia, BAN Almirante Zar and BAM Rio Gallegos air bases on the South American mainland for the reconnaissance and pathfinder roles. One of the Learjet 35A aircraft was shot down over Pebble Island by a Sea Dart missile from the destroyer HMS *Exeter* on 7 June.

14

Lockheed L-188PF Electra, Serial Number: D730, 1 Escuadrilla de Sostén Logístico Móvil, Comando de la Aviación Naval Argentina

In December 1973 the Argentine navy received three ex-civil examples of the Lockheed L-188A Electra four-turboprop transport (later supplemented by one more machine as a source of spares). The aircraft were converted in Argentina to L-188PF utility transport configuration, and in 1982 were on the strength of the 1 Escuadrilla de Sostén Logístico Móvil, based at BAM Rio Grande in Tierra del Fuego, for the transport role.

15

Westland Lynx Mk 23, Serial Number: 3-H-42, 1 Escuadrilla de Helicopteros, Comando de la Aviación Naval Argentina

The Argentine naval air command ordered a total of 10 Westland Lynx helicopters. The two machines delivered in September 1978 were Mk 23 machines, but the subsequent eight Mk 87 helicopters were never delivered. The two Mk 23 helicopters were operated by 1 Escuadrilla de Helicópteros for deployment on the 'Type 42' destroyers ARA *Hércules* and ARA *Santísima Trinidad,* but during the Falklands war were often flown from shore bases such as BAN Puerto Belgrano. The helicopter serialled 3-H-42 was destroyed on 2 May when it hit the *Santísima Trinidad.*

16

Shorts Skyvan 3M-400-7, Serial Number: PA-52, Prefectura Naval Argentina

PA-52 was the third of five Shorts Skyvan 3M-400-7 utility transport aircraft delivered to the Prefectura Naval Argentina (Argentine naval agency, or coastguard) in June and July 1971. With their STOL field capability, the aircraft were well suited to the communications role within the occupied Falkland Islands and for light transport between mainland bases and the islands, where their primary operating bases were BAM Malvinas (Port Stanley) and Pebble Island. Two of the five aircraft were deployed to the Falkland Islands, both being lost in the course of the war (one to a naval bombardment of Port Stanley racecourse during 3/4 May and the other to an SAS attack on Pebble Island during 15 May).

COLOUR SECTION

1

The primary warplane providing a defensive capability as the ships of the British task force approached the Falkland Islands, and then a combined offensive and defensive capability after troops had landed on East Falkland, was the Sea Harrier FRS.Mk 1. Such a warplane is seen here as it departs the upward-sloped 'ski jump' forward end of the flight deck of an 'Invincible' class light aircraft carrier. Also visible in the photograph are a Sea King helicopter with the blades of its main rotor folded and, added after the end of the Falklands war, a white-domed Phalanx close-in weapon system mounting carrying a 20-mm six-barrel cannon for the defeat of air targets close to the ship.

2

Long-range air operations drew heavily on the Royal Air Force's inflight-refuelling capability based on the Victor K.Mk 2, an example of which is seen here while refuelling a Harrier GR.Mk 3.

3

The 'Type 42' class destroyer HMS *Coventry* lists to port as she burns after being hit on 25 May by three 1,000-lb (454-kg) bombs from the A-4C Skyhawk flown by Primer Teniente Velasco of Grupo 4. The ship was abandoned 27 minutes later and about one hour after this capsized and sank.

4

Equipped with modern electronic systems including capable electronic support measures in the form of the Loral ARI.18240/1 system in place of the Nimrod MR.Mk 1's Thomson-CSF system, the Nimrod MR.Mk 2 was ideally suited to the task of finding and identifying any of the Argentine navy's warships that might be at sea and thus threatening the ships of the British task force. The aircraft were soon upgraded to Nimrod MR.Mk 2P standard with an inflight-refuelling probe above the forward fuselage to provide the capability for still longer range.

5

In common with a host of other Western-aligned nations, including the United Kingdom, the FAA used the classic C-130 Hercules tactical transport. The prime operator of the type in the Falklands war was Grupo 9. The 10 such aircraft available in April 1982 comprised three, five and two examples of the C-130E, C-130H and KC-130H, the last for the inflight-refuelling role with two underwing hose-and-drogue units. TC-69 was the first of the KC-130H machines, which were delivered in April and May 1979. A C-130 delivered surveillance radar and its operating team to the Falklands on the first day of the Argentine invasion.

6
Seen after the end of the Falklands war, when France allowed the resumption of deliveries, these are seven of the 14 Super Etendard aircraft which the Argentine naval air service eventually received. At the outbreak of hostilities, the service had only five such warplanes and five examples of the Exocet anti-ship missile that was the type's primary weapon.

7
A type which the Royal Navy sorely needed in the Falklands war was an airborne early warning aircraft. An emergency development programme was set in motion to create the Sea King AEW.Mk 2 with Searchwater radar using an antenna in a pressurised fabric radome that was swivelled from the horizontal to the vertical position under the helicopter before the radar was activated, but the type appeared just after the end of hostilities. The lack of any organic AEW capability meant the adoption of the radar picket ship concept, which led to the loss of HMS *Sheffield* and HMS *Coventry.*

8
Only very limited use was made of 'smart' or guided bombs in the Falklands war, these being 'dumb' or conventional free-fall weapons on the deck of HMS *Hermes* before being loaded on Harrier warplanes.

9
Somewhat epitomising the lull before the storm, these aircraft are (from left to right) a Wessex HU.Mk 5, Sea Harrier FRS.Mk 1 and Sea King on the flying platform of the assault ship HMS *Intrepid* during May 1982.

10
With its crew in an inflatable raft and flotation bags helping to keep it above the water, this is a Sea King HAS.Mk 5 helicopter that had to ditch in the south Atlantic.

11
Against the backdrop of terrain typical of East Falkland, Argentine personnel examine the cratering of the runway at BAM Malvinas (Stanley Airport) caused by a single 1,000-lb (454-kg) bomb hit in the first 'Black Buck' mission by a Vulcan B.Mk 2 bomber flying from Ascension Island.

12
Men of the 2nd Battalion The Scots Guards prepare to embark in a Sea King helicopter on the improved flight platform on the adapted cruise liner *Queen Elizabeth 2.*

13
A Chinook HC.Mk 1 helicopter lifts a Wessex HAS.Mk 3 anti-submarine and utility transport helicopter, less its main rotor blades, from the flight platform of a 'County' class destroyer.

14
The last moments of HMS *Antelope's* sinking are recorded on camera on 24 May.

15
The burned out destroyer *HMS Sheffield* wallows in the sea before being taken in tow but capsizing and sinking on 10 May.

16
With a landing craft and the 'Type 42' destroyer HMS *Exeter* alongside and a Sea King helicopter above her in Falkland Sound, this is the RFA *Blue Rover,* a 'Rover' class small fleet tanker and supply vessel of the Royal Fleet Auxiliary.

17
The journey south from the United Kingdom first to Ascension Island and then the Falkland Islands was characterised by great aerial activity not only as the Sea Harrier warplanes practised their role but also as helicopters (such as these Sea King machines on and above the aircraft carrier HMS *Hermes)* completed the laborious but essential task of cross-deck movement to ensure that the right men and equipment were accommodated on the right ships.

18
Having started the Falklands war with yellow markings on the fins of its A-4C warplanes, Grupo 4 changed later in the war to blue markings.

19
Despite its failure in the Falklands war, the IA-58A Pucará remains an effective warplane in the counter-insurgency role.

GLOSSARY

AEW	Airborne Early Warning
ARA	Armada Reppublica Argentina
BAM	Base Aérea Militar
BAN	Base Aérea Naval
CANA	Comando de la Aviación Naval Argentina
CAP	Combat Air Patrol
EA	Estacion Aéronaval
EEC	European Economic Community
FAA	Fuerza Aérea Argentina
HMS	Her Majesty's Ship
LSL	Landing Ship Logistic
NATO	North Atlantic Treaty Organisation
RAF	Royal Air Force
RFA	Royal Fleet Auxiliary
SAS	Special Air Service
SBS	Special Boat Service
STUFT	Ships Taken Up From Trade
V/STOL	Vertical/Short Take Off and Landing

INDEX

References to illustrations are shown in **bold**.
Colour Plates and Colour Section illustrations are prefixed 'pl.' and 'cs.', with page and caption locators in brackets.